MONEY

CHRONICLE$

Bardolf & Company

MONEY CHRONICLE$
A Black Man's Odyssey to Financial Freedom

ISBN 978-1-7356502-4-1
Copyright © 2023 by Carlos A. Lock

Published by Bardolf & Company
  www.bardolfandcompany.com

Cover design by *shawcreativegroup.com*

Author photo by Athena Lock

To my grandparents,

Ennis Lock and Amanda Jean Lock
and
William Simmons and Mary Lena Simmons.

If we command our wealth, we shall be rich and free.
If our wealth commands us, we are poor indeed.

— Edmund Burke

MONEY

CHRONICLE$

A Black Man's Odyssey to Financial Freedom

Carlos A. Lock

Bardolf & Company
Sarasota, Florida

CONTENT$

$ $ $ $ $

You are where you are today because you stand on somebody's shoulders. And wherever you are headed, you cannot get there by yourself. If you stand on the shoulders of others, you have a reciprocal responsibility to live your life so that others may stand on your shoulders. It's the quid pro quo of life. We exist temporarily through what we take, but live forever through what we give.

—Vernon Jordan

Introduction

FINANCIAL LE$$ON$ LEARNED AND NOT LEARNED

Money has always been important to me. Thinking about it often occupies the forefront of my mind. I've fretted about it, spent it, saved it, and wasted it. I've taken care of my family's finances as best I know how, but for many years there was no real rhyme or reason to my buying or saving decisions. I like to splurge on impulse (more on that later). However, I am always prepared for a drought or a rainy day.

There is a well-known saying, often attributed to the Buddha: "When the student is ready, the teacher will appear."

In my case, that happened when I read J. L. Collins' book *The Simple Path to Wealth: Your Road Map to Financial Independence and a Rich, Free Life*. The book was a wake-up call for me. I learned I'm not investing enough to be on the road to financial freedom. Also, it got me thinking about my personal and financial journey, with all the foolishness and pitfalls along the way, and how I can do better with my money.

I want to share some of that with others.

According to a National Housing Conference (NHC) report, 54% of the U.S. population lives paycheck to paycheck. The figures are worse for African Americans. The elderly are disproportionately affected as well. That's a big deal! Think about it: More than half of the population in this country is only a few hundred dollars away from poverty and homelessness. This book serves as a rallying cry for folks to get their financial affairs in order, especially parents who want to give their kids a head start.

In many ways, I have lived the American Dream. Coming from a poor, working-class background, I now enjoy a comfortable middle-class life with my family. And I hope to create a legacy so that my daughters can have as good or better a life than me.

I decided to write this book to clarify my thinking—nothing like clearing your head than putting things on paper—and to help others by sharing my financial journey. In considering it, I realized that my personal and financial journey has been unusual.

I served 20 years, three months, and 23 days in the U.S. Army and retired a Lieutenant Colonel. The benefits that I can leverage from my career to this day are a privilege not afforded to your average American citizen. Only 1% of the U. S. population serves in the military. As a veteran, I have an elite status. Medical coverage, life insurance, pension, and VA loans are just a few benefits from my service. The expectation of officers to be go-getters translated to my ensuring that my finances were squared away when I retired.

If my military career provided me with some benefits and advantages, being a member of a minority, a Black man, has given me a distinct perspective regarding money matters. But while some of my experiences and attitudes may differ from other Americans, I have seen many of my fellow soldiers, friends, and acquaintances deal with the same issues, make the same mistakes, and suffer the consequences as I have. Some chapters and lessons speak specifically to my black experience. Others apply to everyone.

I originally wanted to title this book, *Black Folks and the Money They Ain't Got* because I thought it was catchy and funny and reflected my experience. It's always perplexing when I see *my* people spend more money on their wants than their needs. It happens all the time with my family and friends. They would rather spend money on hair, nails, shoes, or outfits than vehicle repairs or home upgrades. But someone advised me that the title might be offensive to some, unfairly singling out black folks and blaming the victim. The deck has been stacked against Black folks struggling to create wealth for far too long in this country, but that's another book. As I started writing, I realized I needed to look at the man in the mirror, and what I saw regarding my personal finances wasn't as pretty a picture as I'd imagined. So, I'll be the first to admit that I must remove the speck from my eye before I can chastise my brothers and sisters about their money habits.

This book, then, is more about me than others, although I hope it will serve some good to anyone in pursuit of the "American Dream." More importantly, I hope it can act as a wake-up call for others to put their finances in order and enjoy life at the same time.

Looking back on my personal and financial journey so far, I have learned some important and valuable lessons. Some of them took me several times to appreciate and make my own, some I'm still struggling to apply. I hope you'll do better than me.

Carlos A. Lock
January 2023

The illiterate of the 21st century will not be those who cannot read or write, but those who cannot learn, unlearn, and relearn.

— Alvin Toffler

Chapter 1

FIR$T LE$$ON

When I was 12 years old, I accompanied my dad to a Ford dealership in Jackson, Mississippi, to cosign a loan for his younger brother. The place was on the west side of town, and one of our neighbors was a big-time car salesman for the company. The car was a 1988, sky-blue Thunderbird. I don't remember how long my uncle owned the vehicle. When he could no longer maintain the payments, my dad had to cover the loan. He secured the car and parked it in our driveway, but it did not stay there long. It got repoed and returned to the dealership. I'm not sure why my dad didn't try to keep up the payments. I imagine it was more of a burden than he could shoulder. With the mortgage on our home, his truck payments, and the monthly household bills, an additional vehicle created an excessive financial strain. It was, a luxury he couldn't afford.

There were consequences which affected our family's finances and lingered for several years. The charge-off for the Thunderbird appeared on my dad's credit report and ruined his credit rating. As a result, he could not borrow money at a favorable rate. When my mom's 1977 Mercury Cougar was on its last wheels, my dad wanted to get her a good-sized car. But he could only muster the funds for a 1991 Mercury Tracer. It was a serviceable vehicle, not a bad car, but it was small.

Unfortunately, there is no amount of money my uncle could have paid to remedy that situation. I can still hear him apologizing to my dad, who took it in stride. If it had been me in my dad's shoes, I would have sucker punched him, even though that wouldn't have solved anything.

I learned my first financial lesson at a very young age:

> **Never cosign a loan with anyone,**
> **especially a family member.**

As Collins wrote in his book, "… don't cosign with anyone that is fiscally irresponsible." I would extend that to most family members. Just because they stir up a lot of emotions in you, and could use your John Hancock to get ahead, it doesn't mean that they will uphold their end of the bargain. The only exception I would make is for your children. But if you cosign on a car for them, make sure you are the primary owner. That is a way to build credit for them.

As fate would have it, in 1996 I needed a car for my sophomore year at Hampton University. I worked over the summer at a steel foundry in Walterboro, South Carolina. While I learned the importance of hard work, I also knew I was not going to spend my future there. I could not wait to return to school. I made $7.05 per hour, less than the regular employees because I was a part-timer. The company hired me and other summer workers to keep wages low. In addition, the temp agency that coordinated the job took its cut, so I managed to save only about $2,000.

At the end of the summer, my dad and I went to the local Nissan Dealership to procure a vehicle for me. I had read the car ads and a Nissan Sentra was on sale for $11,999.99. I knew I could afford that. What I didn't know about were the finance charges, taxes, and title fees. The sticker price quickly ballooned to $19,000, and my down payment of $2K was merely a drip towards the cost of the car. As a result, I became the cosigner for a 1996 Nissan Sentra with my dad. I think the interest rate was 19% or 20%, and the terms were 60 months (5 years). Not the best of deals, but at least I had reliable wheels. Fortunately, my dad made the payments because I didn't make enough money at school to keep them up myself. When I graduated in 1999, he turned the responsibility over to me.

I promised myself that car loan would be the only time I ever cosigned anything, and I'm glad to say, I have stuck to that decision.

$ $ $ $ $

My father and mother.

Chapter 2

POOR AND DE$TITUTE

I come from a three-generation military family. My paternal grandfather fought in the Second World War. The only other thing I know about him is that he died in a tree accident when my father was five years old. Those are the only two things I ever heard about him: World War II Army veteran and death by tree. Although my grandmother and he were married, it seemed that she had forfeited her rights to his assets—the home and the land. It was the mid-1950s. So, she returned to her parents in Louisiana with her five children. Later, she moved several times throughout the South and had six more children before settling in Jackson, Mississippi. As far as I know, she never remarried. I'm sure she had other jobs, but she mostly earned her living as a cook. She never owned a home or a car, but she raised her seven boys and four girls as a single mom. Besides love and life lessons, she didn't have much of a legacy to leave them.

I remember her as a sweet, loving woman. During my sophomore year of college, she relocated to Hampton with my aunt. Her home-cooked meals made my college life so much easier. There was always something on the stove when I visited her—fried chicken, collard greens, macaroni and cheese, and my favorite—red beans and rice. After letting me eat my fill, she would answer my questions about the family which filled in a lot of gaps. Sometime before she died, she gave me a vintage photo of my dad in his uniform and my mom in her high school graduation cap and gown.

My dad was her third child. I am pretty sure he grew up with no recollection of his father. If he had any memories, he never shared them with my brother and me. On one occasion, he tried to explain the location of my grandfather's gravesite. When I went there, I was struck that all the headstones were inscribed with the Lock name. Some of my relatives had lived a full life, others only a couple of years. I hoped that my ancestors would help me to locate the spot where my grandfather was buried, but I trooped through that cemetery for over an hour and never did.

My dad served in the Army during the Vietnam War and earned a Purple Heart. He never discussed his time in the military. When I was 11, the two of us went to a movie, *Hamburger Hill*. The film was made in 1987 and told the story of an intense, brutal battle during that war. I did not realize it then, but know now my dad wanted the movie to speak for him. He wasn't a very talkative guy.

As a young man, I wanted to be a truck driver like him. Sometimes, he would take me to the company's terminal yard to help clean his truck and let me drive around, but that was the extent of it. I wanted him to teach me something,

We weren't dirt poor—we always had enough to get by—but we weren't rolling in dough. Our disposable income was nonexistent, but my dad always made sure that we had what we needed. Our lights were always on, we had food in refrigerator and clothes on our backs.

As I got older, I wanted money to buy things that caught my fancy, but my parents routinely refused my requests. That spawned my attitude toward money. I figured that if I had my own money, no one could ever tell me No.

Because I worked throughout high school at McDonald's, I always had money to do the stuff I wanted to do. Unfortunately,

I was unbanked, meaning—I did not have a bank account or any savings. However, the McDonald's sent its daily deposits to a bank, and my manager directed me there to get my paychecks cashed at no charge. I always spent what I earned.

In June of 1990 my brother joined the Army Reserves to fund his college education. We thought he was going to get called up during the Gulf War, but he never did. He served several years in the reserves until his commitment ended.

It was a forgone conclusion that I would go to college although I was not sure where. I would get flyers and brochures in the mail all the time with information about military colleges. My dad would leave them in my room, but joining Uncle Sam's Army was the furthest thing from my mind at that point.

After attending a summer program at Hampton University in 1994, I decided I wanted to go there. That's when I realized that, financially, we were in the vicinity of broke to poor. Hampton is expensive, so my dad had to borrow money for me to attend. He took out an education loan of $35,000 that paid for my first two years there. It was a strain on him. He never said anything, but I had a pretty good idea that he was robbing Peter to pay Paul, just enough each month to keep creditors at bay.

It never dawned on me that my parents could not afford my college education. Had I known that, I might have chosen a lower cost school and would have saved more of the checks from McDonald's. However, it was close to the end of the school year, and by then Hampton University was my only option. Time was of the essence. As a brash 18-year-old, I could only think of myself and what I felt the world owed me.

In retrospect, I wish my dad had been clear with me about his situation, but no conversations about family finances ever took place in my parents' household. Their attitude was: it's not for you to worry about. That is still true in most American homes.

While I didn't take a financial lesson from that experience at the time, it has affected the way I deal with my children. I believe that families should set aside time to go over financial books, no later than when a child enters high school. So, I discuss all family money matters with my two daughters, Chassidy and Camille, regardless of their ability to retain the information or understand how it applies to their current lives. I don't make them take tests or quizzes, but I repeat the same messages at every opportunity.

For example, if our mortgage increases, I break down the principal, taxes and insurance so they have an idea of how home ownership works. In fact, I have reviewed all of our family's assets under my control with them.

If your kids are anything like mine, they think dental visits are free because they don't see any money change hands at the conclusion of their visit. This provides me the opportunity to discuss health care and dental insurance. I know it seems like a lot to put on the shoulders of adolescents, but given our current financial environment, it is necessary. I don't want them to take things for granted. In America, it makes a big difference if your job/career offers a decent health care plan that covers most medical expenses. Unfortunately, even with the Affordable Care Act, too many people, even if they work have little to no health care coverage and cannot afford a visit to the doctor when they get sick.

For my daughters, knowing their financial situation is key to making buying decisions. Chassidy and Camille receive money for birthdays, getting good grades, their weekly allowance, or just for being who they are. I require them to always save a portion, even if it's just a few dollars—my attempt to instill a habit that will benefit their future. Both have their own checking and savings accounts so they can purchase things they want. I often talk to them about the difference between wants and needs because we provide for all their needs. I also tell them, "Do better in school. Invest at an earlier age."

Hopefully, these conversations will show them that money matters and make them more financially savvy than I was. If they can avoid some of the pitfalls I tumbled into, starting with college, it will have been worth it.

As I mentioned, my dad assumed education loans to pay for my first two years at Hampton University. I earned an Army ROTC scholarship to cover the last two years and took on an additional loan of $7,000 to cover other miscellaneous bills.

I also fell victim to predatory credit card companies and banks that lurk on college campuses. Nations Bank, now Bank of America, huckleberried a credit card on me during my first semester of school. A bank representative stopped me on the way to the dining hall and asked if my parents sent me money. When I said Yes, he immediately offered to sign me up. I completed the paperwork and received my credit card. When I quickly maxed it out, I signed up for more. That started me on my journey into indebtedness during my college years. Like many others, I was too young and inexperienced to know better.

In 1998 during my junior year of college, I learned an important life lesson, though, when I took the annual fitness test for Army ROTC. I had to meet the required physical standards to retain my scholarship. On the day of the test, there was a heavy rainstorm, and it was hard to focus, with the strong winds and the rain pelting my face, and I failed the running part. My poor showing puzzled the instructors because of my physique. I stood six feet tall, weighed 170 pounds, and looked the part of an athlete, but the run got the best of me. The truth of the matter was I hated running and hadn't work on my own to improve.

The scholarship covered the last two years of school, and Army ROTC was critical for me to complete my degree. I had no other means to fund my education. Fortunately, one of the instructors gave me good counsel for the 30 days I had to prepare for the re-test. I was working at Super K-Mart and spending my spare time on campus. But during the next month, I skipped spring break and made time to run with different instructors every day. On weekends, I ran on my own. I learned that running was more mental than physical. It was the principle of mind over matter to deal with any discomfort and pain. While I didn't ace the second test, my time improved enough so that running was no longer an issue for me. Not then and not throughout my Army career.

I realized that one must put in extra work when performance is lacking. I understood that forgoing extracurricular activities was necessary to achieve my goals. Running, extra work, and sacrifice became my response to life's challenges as I prepared to enter the Army.

$ $ $ $ $

Chapter 3

BORROWING/LOANING/ GIVING MONIE$

In Shakespeare's play *Hamlet*, Polonius counsels his son Laertes who is going away to study abroad, "Neither a borrower or a lender be." Although Polonius is a pompous fool, that's good financial advice. Not always easy to follow, though.

The last time I borrowed money directly (other than via credit cards) was in 1999. Throughout my college years at Hampton University, I was always running late and parked illegally to get to class. I would leave my 1996 Nissan Sentra in spaces reserved for faculty and administrators. Sometimes there would be a ticket waiting for me on the windshield, but most of the time I got away with it. I didn't bother to pay any of the fines. I'm happy to report that I have changed my ways—the military made sure of that. Nowadays, I arrive at a meeting or appointment 15 minutes early, with plenty of time to find a legal parking space. In hindsight, I wish my 47-year-old self could have talked some sense into 22-year-old Carlos then. Not that my younger self would have listened.

In May of 1999, a week before graduation, I had a rude awakening while visiting the financial office. All those parking fines had added up and been charged to my student account. I wouldn't be allowed to graduate until I settled the bill. I didn't know what to do. I owed about $400 in parking fees and was dead broke. All my credit cards were maxed out.

I didn't want to ask my parents for money—they were en route to my graduation from Mississippi. I didn't think my brother could help. None of my college buddies had that amount of cash on hand. I finally approached my aunt, who worked at the university, and told her about my trouble. She gave me the money along with a stern look. I thanked her and promised I would repay her in a timely manner. Then I rushed to the finance office to clear my debt.

Although I was glad to resolve my financial worries, I was also down on myself. So, I contacted my girlfriend's mother, LPJ— her name was Linda Person Joiner, but I always called her by her initials. She'd taken a shine to me, and I used to talk to her every day during my last semester of school. When I told her about my financial woes, she said I shouldn't worry. At graduation, she gave me the money to pay back my aunt, which I did. That was a good thing. But now, I felt indebted to my girlfriend's mother.

LPJ undoubtedly helped me because I was dating her daughter. However, when I ended that relationship a year after graduation, she did not want the money back and made it clear she would not take it if I tried to repay her. LPJ is kind and has a big heart, and she saw something in me. She was a pivotal person in my life, and I never forgot her generosity. I have kept in touch with her and we occasionally speak on the telephone. Several years ago, LPJ was battling cancer, and I visited her while she was recovering. When I entered the hospital room, she and her husband were all smiles. It was like meeting old friends.

Which brings me to my belief that there are two ways to repay people's generosity: Pay it back or pay it forward.

In this instance, I paid it forward. I graduated, went into the Army and made something of myself. I am sure LPJ would say that the $400 was money well spent.

The first time I tried to pay it forward didn't turn out so well, though. When I purchased a used 1994 Acura Legend, I gave my Nissan Sentra to the daughter of my favorite aunt. The car was paid for. It was only five years old and had less than 100,000 miles on the odometer. My cousin was pregnant and didn't have a way to get around by herself, so the Sentra helped her out a lot. Sometime later, during a family gathering, she refused when I asked her to go to the store for me and pick up some beer. I was livid, so angry that I wanted the keys back to my car. After cooling down, I realized that my cousin was not interested in paying it forward and let it go. A couple years later, she tried to trade the Sentra in. I was very disappointed in her and never did anything for her again.

It has been said that, if you loan someone money, it will be the beginning of the end of the relationship, especially when it comes to a family member. Obviously, the same goes for giving someone an unsolicited present.

Sometime later, when my aunt mentioned that her refrigerator was not working, I was doing OK financially and told her to go to an appliance store and pick out the one she wanted. I would send her the money. She was my favorite aunt on my mom's side because she treated me like her son. She always encouraged me, and most importantly, empowered me by treating me like a responsible person. I trusted her and would have done anything for her.

When she'd made her choice, I sent her the money—more than $500. We both understood that it was not a loan but a present. After a few days, I called her to inquire about the refrigerator, but she avoided answering my question. A couple of months later, I visited her, and the same old refrigerator stood in her kitchen. She hadn't bought a new one. On top of that, she refused to tell me what she had used the money for. Again, I was livid, having failed to learn from the previous situation. I fumed for a while and, remembering my experience with her daughter and the Nissan Sentra, thought: The apple didn't fall far from the tree. That was the last time that I ever did anything for my aunt as well. (I still have a favorite aunt on my father's side.)

Because it was the second time I got burned, I realized that it was my fault. My assumptions and expectations were unreasonable. That taught me an important lesson that I live by to this day:

> **When you give something to others,**
> **it belongs to them to do with as they please.**

It took me a while to get comfortable with that approach, but I managed to do it. If someone needs something and I want them to have it, I make the purchase myself. That way I know where the money went.

It's crucial to remove feelings from any money decisions, even if it isn't always easy to do so. When friends or relatives need something, they are going to play on your emotions. They will continue to come at you because they know you have the money. You are their number one target. But you are no longer their priority after you make the loan. They say to themselves, "He doesn't really want or need his money back!" Asking them for it or reminding them that they are still delinquent often leads to confrontations, with the borrower acting out and using outrage to deflect their lack of responsibility. You don't want that kind of hassle.

The best way not to get into such a situation is to avoid it in the first place. Make it a habit not to act like a bank and lend money to others. I am not talking about amounts less than $50. I loaned out that kind of money in high school and college and had to borrow those sums myself to get by.

But I decline most other requests for money. One of my relatives wanted me to loan him $5,000. It happened that I was getting ready for a flight en route to a deployment to Afghanistan, and dealing with money was the furthest thing from my mind. I told him so, and he didn't push the issue. Another relative asked me for $30,000 for a "business opportunity." I acted polite like I was listening, but once I heard that figure, I didn't pay attention anymore. I respectfully declined and directed him to try his luck with another family member.

It's OK to say no without giving a reason. I also use the excuse "I can't. I just paid the government a boat load of money in taxes." The mention of taxes renders everyone silent, especially folks that don't pay them.

$ $ $ $ $

There are three kinds of people:
the haves, the have-nots, and
the have-not-paid-for-what-they-haves.

— Earl Wilson

Chapter 4

PO$T COLLEGE

Although I managed to graduate college on time, I had a lot of credit card debt. I wasn't alone in that department. Many of my fellow graduates were saddled with large monthly interest and repayment bills, too. I carried seven credit cards, including one to put gas in my car. Altogether I owed about $17,500 in addition to my college loans. Believe me, I know and understand the despair that one feels about being mired in debt.

Which brings me to another aspect of post-college indebtedness—student loans and loan forgiveness.

I know pundits are down on folks taking out student loans to attend college. It's a frequent topic on blogs and podcasts. I can see the pros and cons. However, I don't think people should be attacked for going into debt in pursuit of a college degree. I understand it might seem like a bad financial deal if you don't attend college to become a teacher, doctor, or lawyer. But the "experts" don't give enough credence to the value of the experience. Some folks meet their wives in college, others join fraternities and develop lifelong bonds with their fellow "Greeks." I am not sure what my career path would have been had I not attended Hampton University. The friends I met there and the experiences I had broadened my outlook on life.

At the same time, there is no denying that student loan debt holds back many graduates for a long time, putting them into a deep financial hole at a point in their lives when they should be building for their future. The website *Nerdwallet.com* reports that, as of 2022, 43 million Americans carry student loan debt totaling more than $1.6 trillion. According to a 2022 *Forbes* magazine article, the average student loan debt is $28,950.

As of this writing, President Biden has promised debt forgiveness of $10,000 to $20,000 for many students carrying college loans, although the program has stalled in the courts. When the president made the promise part of his 2020 election campaign, it sparked heated discussions about whether or not to help graduates burdened by debt and broke. The advocates suggested students should not be punished for trying to realize the American Dream—a better life, home ownership, and disposable income—through education. At the time, a Facebook post caught my attention which showed a poster insisting that student loans should be restructured to reduce interest rates and term lengths. I think that is prudent and fair.

I haven't supported student loan forgiveness because it's akin to reparations for slavery to me. There is no way to compensate a particular group at another group's expense. And what about the disciplined and diligent students who paid off their loans as required? What do we get? I was one of those borrowers who honored his commitment. When you borrow money, you pay it back. Forgiving student loans only impedes borrowers from doing the right thing. I did not think the loans my father took out were predatory, but many feel theirs are and are advocating that something be done.

When you argue against student loan forgiveness, some folks think that you are insensitive. I have a conservative stance on this matter. It's an emotional trigger for me because I have been in debt up to my neck and saddled with student loans as well. I went without vacations, dining out and other luxuries to take care of my payments.

When I was on rest and recuperation (R and R) leave from Afghanistan, I visited with my mom and dad, and my brother's family. My parents were divorced but everyone gathered at our childhood home. I was drinking and having a good time with family. I don't know how it came up, but my mom made a comment that she paid for me to go to Hampton. I responded as if stung by a bee, "Like hell you did." At that point, the good times were gone. My brother blames the alcohol for my outburst which is partially true because it sometimes magnifies my reactions. Also, I keep emotions bottled up, so when the dam breaks, years of frustration come pouring out, not my feelings about the issue at hand. (I don't consider myself a hot head, but I admit having my moments.)

What my mom didn't know was that I paid off the student loans that my dad had assumed. Because of health issues he could no longer work regularly as a truck driver. He didn't talk about it with anyone, but it came up in one of our conversations that he had not been on the road for a few months. My dad would never ask for help—he has his pride—but I told him to send me the student loan bill. I was happy to take something off his plate. I figured after nearly 15 years, the amount due would be around $15,000. Boy, was I wrong. My dad took out forbearances and paid only the monthly minimum. As a result, the money owed was close to the original loan. I was shocked, angry, and upset—I did not sign up for that—but, once I recovered, I decided to stay the course. It was the right thing to do. But I didn't process how I felt about it—hence the blow-up at my mom.

About three months after that conversation, I received orders to deploy to Afghanistan. With my combat pay bonus and my regular Army pay, I had the cash to pay the entire amount of the student loan. But I didn't want to do that. My wife Athena and two daughters, who were toddlers at the time, would be at home, and I wanted a cushion for them during my absence. So, I obtained a Certificate Deposit loan to pay off the education loan.

My mom didn't know any of this, and I felt bad for blowing up at her. Since then, I have made peace with her.

> **It's not a good idea to let emotions run roughshod over family and friends.**

Paying off the loan was not a badge of honor on my part or a comeuppance on my dad. I was just shocked for a while that the loan was still the original amount.

So, I understand the anguish student loan debt can cause and how it can affect people mentally and emotionally. It's hard to smile when you're not making a dent in what you owe. But still, I don't completely support student loan forgiveness—it does not create financial discipline. I remember my college days when some of my peers looked forward to receiving student loan refunds. In those days, these loans were more a guestimate, it wasn't like borrowing for a home or a car, where you'd receive the exact amount. Sometimes, there were extra funds left over after the disbursement. Some of my classmates went on shopping sprees, others took spring break trips to Jamaica and Mexico, and when the program didn't go through, ended up stuck with additional bills if there was no refund.

I do support restructuring student loans to a more favorable rate so folks can see the light at the end of the financial tunnel.

While I am diligent when repaying loans and don't believe one should wait on legislation to forgive personal debt, the real lesson here is:

> **Keep your cool during conflicts with others.**

To be honest, though, I still have difficulties applying that lesson in my personal life.

$ $ $ $ $

I don't know why I left
But I must've done wrong,
And it won't be long
Till I get on back home.
Sat me in that barber's chair,
Spun me around, I had no hair;.
Used to drive a Cadillac,
Now I back it on my back.
Used to drive a limousine,
Now I'm wearing Army green.
Used to date a beauty queen,
Now I date my M16.

— Army Marching Cadence

Chapter 5

JOINING UNCLE SAM'$ ARMY

When I entered the U.S. Army as a Second Lieutenant in 1999, I was temporarily assigned to Aberdeen Proving Grounds, Maryland for officer training. I had no clue what I signed up for, but my financial situation improved immediately. Besides having health care and life insurance taken care of, I lived in furnished quarters, ate discounted meals and, most importantly, received bi-monthly paychecks.

I quickly learned to appreciate the words "per diem." Because the assignment was temporary, I received a daily allowance, paid in a monthly lump sum, in addition to my regular earnings. That windfall lasted from June to October 1999 and was the most money I made until then. The excitement was short-lived, though, because all the creditors from my college years wanted their money. I felt like I was being bled dry because my income consumed most of my debt payments. I kept hemorrhaging money.

Fortunately, my debts didn't impact my status in the Army. I had no difficulty obtaining the required security clearance for my commission as an officer. Some candidates are disqualified because of the large amount of money they owed. The Army's position is that service members with significant debt are vulnerable to blackmail by foreign governments.

There is a saying "The Army is people, and the people is Army," which means that while the military is an outfit with regulations, medals and symbols, it's the individuals serving that give it life. Soldiers and officer candidates are ordinary, regular folks that signed up to wear the uniform. Just because they took an oath to serve their country does not make them savvy in other aspects of their lives, be it money or relationships. However, some are knowledgeable. Throughout my years of service, I encountered subordinates, peers, and superiors who were generous with advice and showed me techniques how to manage my finances.

One of my classmates at the officer basic training course talked to me about investing in mutual funds. When I told him I didn't think I was smart enough or had enough money to do so, he reassured me "Carlos it's only a $100 a month." So, I contacted United Services Automobile Association and started an automatic draft of $100 a month from my paycheck for a mutual fund. I didn't do any research. I informed the financial representative that I was a novice investor and favored a conservative approach, and I followed his recommendation. It was one of the best decisions I ever made. On two occasions, I withdrew a significant portion of the money accrued. The first time was to rehab a rental property when I needed the cash to pay the contractor. The second time was for the down payment on a house to relocate my mom to South Carolina. I still contribute $100 monthly to this fund, and it has grown steadily over the years.

> **If you can, invest a portion, however small, in a mutual fund or equivalent.**

Another classmate suggested I shop around for car insurance rates, rather than remain with the company my family had used for years. I followed his advice and found a better deal.

Taking my military friends and superiors' suggestions made me feel empowered and proud that I was actively participating in my financial affairs.

After graduating from the basic course, I received my first posting at Fort Hood in Texas. I still had credit card and student loan debt, but the financial forest didn't look impenetrable anymore. I could see streaks of sunlight on the other side. I was no longer entitled to per diem payments and my living arrangements and meals became my responsibility. The Army did provide additional basic allowances for housing and subsistence, but because of the debt I carried, I didn't think I could afford to have my own apartment. Also, the idea of living in town didn't sit well with me. Killeen, Texas, where Fort Hood was located, felt like another planet, as strange as I imagined setting foot on Antarctica.

Shortly after I arrived one of the enlisted men asked if I knew what "Killeen" stood for. When I said No, he said, "Kill Each n Every N _____ (you can supply the rest.) in Texas. I was dumbfounded. I had not realized that the place had such a reputation. I had always been aware of my surroundings in Jackson, Mississippi, but now I was on high alert. Historically, Fort Hood had a reputation for not being kind to Black officers. It was there in 1944 that Second Lieutenant Jackie Robinson, who later broke the color barrier in Major League Baseball, faced court martial for refusing to move to the back of a military bus. He was acquitted and filed his retirement papers three weeks later, and was honorably discharged.

By the time I served there, it was more integrated. About 45 percent of the enlisted soldiers and NCOs in my battalion were African American, although, at first, I was the only black commissioned officer assigned to the unit.

The town of Copperas Cove was 15 miles west of Killeen. A lot of soldiers lived there because of Killeen's reputation. Unfortunately, it was in a dry county with heavy police patrols. If you were black, you could be pulled over for the slightest infraction. Copperas Cove reminded me of a southern "sun down town" where you were not welcome after dark if you were an African American. Another town to the east, Harker Heights, was still a developing community and was much nicer than Killeen. The air seemed cleaner, and there were better restaurants.

Fortunately, everything I needed—groceries, fuel, household goods, or clothes—were available on the base. I never attempted to date any of the locals. Although Killeen had a movie theater and a mall, I always went out in Copperas Cove or Harker Heights for entertainment. It took about a year before I felt comfortable in Killeen. After that, we would patronize the local clubs on the weekends. Most of the patrons were either veterans or actively serving so there were no hassles. In retrospect, it may not have been as bad as I imagined, or my vigilance paid off. Despite Killeen's reputation, I never had any issues during my three-year tour.

A couple of my classmates from the basic course were assigned there, too, and we agreed to move in together. Typically, rent/mortgage is the most significant expenditure in people's budget. Since COVID, things have gotten worse, devouring as much as three-quarters of the monthly income of people making $15 an hour. Imagine folks trying to get by who earn even less or don't have a job. I was still broke, but having roommates gave me a social life and allowed me to indulge myself occasionally by eating out at Whataburger, a regional fast food restaurant chain.

The job consumed most of my time, especially during field training exercises. Fort Hood has an expanse of training land, mostly flat and wooded, with some hills. We would move from one spot to another, then return to the motor pool area to clean and account for our equipment. A couple of weeks later, we'd do it all over again. I slept under the Texas stars a lot during those months.

At the time, I was still in a long-distance relationship with LPJ's daughter, so I didn't need an entertainment budget. When we graduated in May of 1999, we decided to continue our relationship despite the distance. She was living in Birmingham, Alabama, and during my basic training, I visited her on three occasions. But when I got transferred to Fort Hood and got busy, I stopped communicating regularly. Before long, we broke up.

During training, there is no need to expend any funds because Uncle Sam provides the fuel, housing, beans, and bullets. I was no longer using my credit cards, but I could only afford the minimal repayments. The story was the same for my student loan. I paid just the monthly minimum. It felt like trying to eat an elephant one bite at a time, or rather, two elephants. I know folks say that is the way to do it—one payment at a time—and they are right. But that doesn't make you feel any better about being debt-ridden.

I learned quickly to be "unfinancial", which means that an officer doesn't discuss his financial situation with anyone, including superiors, peers, or subordinates. Officer's pay is higher than that of enlisted members. On day one of military service, a Second Lieutenant earns significantly more money than a Sergeant First Class with more than 12 years of service and a couple of combat tours under their belt. The Sergeant First Class is a proven commodity while the Second Lieutenant is paid on his or her potential. It may not make sense or be fair, but that is how it is. These pay scales are common knowledge and are no secret to anyone.

Still, you don't want to get into a monetary conversation about it. That only leads to resentment.

As a young officer, I focused on proving my mettle to the more experienced veterans. I wanted to demonstrate that I was worth the paycheck Uncle Sam cut me on the first and fifteenth of every month. I also tried to convince my subordinates by working late, being accessible and always contributing money to support events.

Officers also have additional military duties such as taking care of unit movement and physical security, which are mandated through regulations. There are also special events to coordinate, and the lot usually falls to you when you are a junior lieutenant low on the totem pole. I was the officer in charge for a prayer breakfast and Organizational Day, an annual picnic for every soldier in the unit. My job was coordinating the food, events, and the timeline. We played horseshoes, flag football, and volley ball.

Sometimes the Army does not provide the wherewithal, and you have to be creative to get things done. On my watch, there was a requirement to have a cake for everyone. When I met with the culinary specialists, they informed me that they could make the cake, but I had to pay for the decorative items. As an officer, everything hinges on your ability to accomplish the mission, so I spent my own money to ensure we had a good cake. The event was a success, even though I didn't get a slice. It added to my reputation that Lieutenant Lock could make stuff happen, and I was understandably proud.

Of course, many of the veterans remained unimpressed. I did not realize it then, but there was nothing that I could have done to persuade long-timers that I was worth the better money.

Unlike me, many enlisted men and women were married and had children. They tried to make the most of what they earned, to get ahead while providing for their families back home. That would have been a big enough challenge on its own, but what made it more difficult for them were the predatory practices of the local car dealers, furniture stores, banks, and loan companies.

As far as I was concerned, one of the worst was the Fort Hood National Bank, which catered to all Army personnel. It had several branches on the base, which was convenient. However, the bank's primary purpose was to obtain deposits by any means necessary. Back in those days, if service members established an account with direct deposit, the bank would allow access to their pay about five days before it got wire transferred. In many cases, the soldiers spent the money right away and would be cash strapped by the time they received their pay officially. I had learned my lesson with my college credit cards and made sure to steer clear of this financial institution. But young, inexperienced soldiers figured, "What better place to bank than one with the name of our base." I tried to discourage those in my charge to avoid the bank, but I had only marginal success.

Also, some retired Sergeants Major took jobs with financial companies that sold insurance, investment products, and other financial instruments. They would use the fact that they were trusted and respected as military veterans to ingratiate themselves with newly assigned soldiers and take advantage of them.

I offered advice to the soldiers under my command to avoid financial stumbling blocks and pitfalls as best I could. The base provided a list of banned businesses because of their predatory practices (rent to own, payday loans, car dealerships, massage parlors), but many service members couldn't resist the temptation to enjoy the good life. I cannot count the number of soldiers that were harmed by these companies and caused themselves financial difficulties and ruin. In some cases, the Army discharged them for not being able to meet their financial obligations even though they were victims of predatory companies.

$ $ $ $ $

Chapter 6

BLACK BANK$

I've mentioned several times that banks aren't necessarily your friend when it comes to money matters, and that is true for people of all color. Which brings me to the subject of Black banks. As of this writing, there are 42 such financial institutions in the United States, serving minority communities and at least 51% Black-owned.

However, I consider Black bank or Black-owned bank a misnomer because money is green. (At least in the United States. The paper money of most other countries is a lot more colorful.) And, as technology advances with online banking and crypto currency—however that may shake out—who knows what form money will take in the future. For now, banks as brick-and-mortar financial institutions are here to stay; and over the last few years, there has been much discussion about banking black or providing banking services where most Black folks reside.

Historically, Black people have been ambivalent towards saving money in banks. More than 100 years ago, following the end of slavery during Reconstruction, Black banks were an essential part of achieving freedom and independence. Benevolent societies and churches sprung up and made credit available to fund other projects. In March 1874, Frederick Douglass became the head of Freedman's Savings and Trust Company, a Black institution, in an attempt to restore Black folks' confidence in banking. He even invested $10,000 of his own money. His generous act did not achieve the desired result. The bank closed its doors in June of that same year.

Subsequently, massacres in Wilmington, North Carolina (1898) and Tulsa, Oklahoma (1921) impacted Black folks' outlook on banking. What money they had saved was lost, burned in their homes or in the Black banks in their neighborhoods. In 1964, Freedom National Bank of Harlem was co-founded by Jackie Robinson, the first African-American player in Major League baseball and a national treasure. Unfortunately, that bank shut its doors in 1990 due to insolvency. *

It is against that historical background that Black leaders across the nation have tried to establish easier ways for Black folks to bank. They stress the need to have financial institutions that cater specifically to African Americans. The difficulty is that, while Black banks must be insured by the Federal Deposit Insurance Corporation, many have a low credit rating. As a result, there are limited opportunities to secure a loan from the FDIC in times of financial trouble. In addition, Black banks typically charge higher fees than established financial institutions like Bank of America. High fees tend to have folks seek greener pastures or just keep their money under the mattress.

In 2017, I opened a bank account with a Black bank in Columbus, Georgia. It was a branch of an Atlanta-based bank. Because I sold my mom's house in South Carolina, I had a substantial amount of cash on hand and deposited about $15,000. When my wife, Athena, and I signed the paperwork, the banking representative

---

* Mehrsa Baradaran does an excellent job of providing a historical context for Black banks in her book *The Color of Money: Black Banks and the Racial Wealth Gap.*

did not offer any other options than basic savings, such as a money market account or an account earning a higher interest rate. At the time it didn't bother us because we had no plans to use the funds and were happy to leave them there. Of course, the worst thing you can do with a significant amount of cash is to deposit it in a way that it only earns pennies. But that didn't concern us. We never intended to use that account for any transactions or withdrawals, only deposits, because we felt we were doing a service to the Black community.

I don't carry any change in my pocket, so from time to time, I wrap the coins I collect in my glass jar in paper rolls and take them to the bank. I must have made a couple of $150 deposits to the account that way.

> **Coin change adds up, so collect and deposit**

After a few months passed, during which there were no transactions, I received a noticed that the account was going to be closed due to inactivity. In the meantime, I would be assessed a fee if there were no transactions by the next banking cycle. I was dumbfounded and angry. Here I thought I was doing something for the Black community, but it was a Black institution that tried to stick it to me.

I immediately wrote a check for the entire deposit and emptied the account. There was no way I was going to continue to bank at that place, Black or not. No one from the bank ever reached out to ask why I closed my account. It turned out to be a good thing that I took immediate action because, several months later, that bank branch closed. I don't know what would have happened if my money still had been deposited there, I doubt I'd have seen a penny of it without resorting to legal recourse. I understand the cost of operating a brick-and-mortar financial institution, but there's nothing like walking into a bank and talking to a real person. Times certainly have changed since I had my first job at McDonald's when I could cash my paycheck at the company's bank for no charge. I was 15 years old and unbanked—I did not have a bank account - no one seems to provide that service any longer without a bank account. As a result, Black folks are limited to local mom-and-pop convenience stores, liquor stores or payday loan establishments to cash their checks for a minimum fee of 10%.

Some of these outfits are supposedly backed by established banks like Bank of America and Wells Fargo, but they aren't subject to FDIC or disclosure regulations. Banks must provide full disclosure about transactions and fees. They can be penalized by the Feds if they venture too far from their guidelines. Payday loan and rent-to-own places are not regulated. That's why they can engage in predatory practices. It takes local legislation to limit their number, location and business methods. But folks need this money bad. Many of them are being paid under the table so they are not going to raise an issue. That money barely gets them through the week, so they have to keep going to do it all over again. The folks that employ them keep their own proceeds in reputable bank accounts and take advantage of the unbanked workers.

There is a lot of clamoring for Black banks to address these issues, but what do we really expect from such institutions? It boils down to proximity. If you are a hard worker, never been laid off and need money for home or a new car, despite your limited credit history, you want a Black bank. If the check cashing place is taking too much of your money, you want a Black bank in your community. But most Black neighborhoods are still redlined because it's risky to put a business in an area of town where crime rates are high, which is the case in most cities across the United States. Thus, Black folks must travel further to bank.

If at all possible, get a bank account

While some banks provide monetary incentives for opening a new account, they also require direct deposits of pay checks. Most folks want control of their money, so they balk at such programs. On the other hand, many don't make a living wage and live month to month, so there is no incentive for them to leave their money in a bank for any length of time.

Unfortunately, the wealth gap will continue to widen as Black folks have limited access to financial institutions and their mindset regarding keeping money in the bank doesn't change. Furthermore, while living pay check to pay check, they are one adverse life situation—hospitalization, eviction, car breakdown—away from being under water. They are part of the "Missing Class": too well-off to be working poor, too at risk to be middle class.

$ $ $ $

There is no romance without finance.

Chapter 7

LOVE AT FIR$T $IGHT

Having learned my lesson in college, I avoided such pitfalls as a young Army officer and kept plugging away to pay down my debts. The turning point came when I deployed to Kuwait for Operation Intrinsic Action from April to August 2001. When the Army sends you overseas, there's additional monetary benefits. Because Kuwait was considered a combat zone, I was entitled to combat tax exclusion, so my income wasn't taxed. Using the extra money, I managed to zero out my charge cards and move my financial status from red to black.

Kuwait was hot, like opening the oven door in a small kitchen without ventilation. We were embedded in the desert about 40 kilometers from the Iraqi border. It was not a combat mission but an operational deployment to give soldiers practical experience and steel their resolve for actual combat. There were still stark reminders from Operation Desert Storm—one of the highways was lined on both sides with the rusted shells of burnt-out military vehicles. Our unit's mission was logistic support to a tank-heavy task force. The M1A2 Abrams tank was the primary combat vehicle we supported. We conducted live-fire maneuvers and monitored the maintenance schedule to ensure that the tanks were fully operational and could "shoot, move, and communicate" at all times. Sometimes, we had to take a tank to the rear when the repairs could not be made at the "battlefront" location.

By then, I had met my future wife, Athena. In the summer of 2000, I was the only African American commissioned officer in the battalion when a white female colleague told me about a black female officer—also a lieutenant—who had been assigned to Charlie Company. Before I laid eyes on her, I called the company headquarters where she worked and asked her out—a true blind date. Athena didn't know anything about me either, but other female service members vouched for me, and she said yes.

Initially, her full lips and breasts caught my attention. But what won me over was her determined, untamable spirit. She'd grown up in Ashburn, a small town in southern Georgia. Her parents never married. As the oldest of five children, she always was responsible for her brothers and sisters. The family moved a lot, and she did not get to have much of a childhood. Still, her mom was very protective of her. For her senior prom, she was not allowed to stay out past 10 p.m. When she left home for Mercer University in Macon, Georgia, she never looked back. Because she was quite smart, she was on an academic scholarship in her first year. Army ROTC financed her last three years. Along the way, Athena joined a sorority, Delta Sigma Theta. She graduated in May of 1999 with a B.S. in Chemistry.

We dated several times before becoming more seriously involved, but we both kept seeing other people. Athena didn't realize how gorgeous she was and did not put much stock in her daily appearance. Her mantra was, "Take me as I am or not at all." I encouraged her to vary her hairstyles and wardrobe and reminded her of her namesake Athena, the patron goddess of the city of Athens in Greece, who was both wise and beautiful.

Because Athena wanted to become a doctor, the Army granted her an educational delay. That meant she did not have to join immediately and gave her time to pursue a medical career. But when she didn't score high enough on the MCAT, she became a Medical Service Officer. After a training stint at Fort Sam Houston in Texas, she reported to Fort Hood to begin her career.

Athena also deployed to Kuwait, and I saw her there every day. Male and female officers shared the same tent, so I woke up in her presence every morning. We usually ate lunch together too. Some nights, we would find a quiet place to spend time and talk. We kept those intimate nights G-rated. Even though we saw each other a lot, I wrote her a daily letter to continue courting her. Occasionally, she wrote me back. Getting mail is a big deal in the Army. It definitely increases morale. The time in Kuwait together intensified our feelings for each other.

In August 2001, when we returned to the States, Athena was assigned as the battalion's Adjutant/Personnel Officer. Her position made her responsible for the paperwork of more than 500 soldiers, which included pay, separations, retirements, awards, promotions, and other official records.

I took two weeks of rest and recuperation leave and visited my family in South Carolina. I was glad to be back in the States and celebrated by exercising my financial freedom, purchasing another car, a 1994 Acura Legend. I jumped back onto the hamster wheel and restarted the cycle of going into debt.

A couple of days before my leave ended, the 9-11 attacks on the World Trade Center and the Pentagon shocked our country to its core. We in the military were angry and eager to retaliate. We'd sworn an oath to defend our country, and we'd been assailed on our very own soil! In times of national crisis, a soldier can be recalled at a moment's notice, and most units went on alert to prepare for potential worldwide deployment. Because our unit had just been in Kuwait, there were rumors that we would return there, but we never received the call. Nor were we sent to Afghanistan to deal with the Taliban. Funds had already been allocated for us to go to the National Training Center (NTC) at Fort Irwin, California, so we maintained our scheduled rotation there from November to December 2001. (NTC works to ready units for large scale combat operations and validates their readiness level by determining if they meet deployability criteria.)

In January of 2002, Athena and I moved in together. There was a lot of love and passion between us. We were homie-lover friends, which meant we were intimate but seeing other people. We were good business partners as well, renting a three-bedroom house and splitting all the bills 50-50. There were never any disagreements. It didn't take long for us to grow close. I don't remember the defining moment, but we decided to be an exclusive couple at some point. I did not propose marriage to Athena right away, but we were in a committed relationship. We went out to dinner and saw a lot of movies. Because Athena likes to cook, we often hosted other officers at our home.

When you start dating, both parties are too busy enjoying each other's company to consider the long-term impact of finances on romance. It's funny how money seems to come in foreign languages when people get together at that nirvana stage of a relationship. Initially, it's Dutch: you pay, I pay. Then it turns into English: you get this one. I'll get the next one. Then it's French: oui oui (we we)—you and I are one, we are partners in this together. That's certainly how Athena and I embarked on our financial journey together. And it's still true in some ways. She always includes me when she plans to use my money and says "we" before asking for my opinion.

When we first became a couple in 2002, Athena wanted to purchase a special car for herself. I asked to accompany her to the dealership, but she refused. So much for a committed relationship. Looking back, I should have realized that it represented in seedling form our future financial arrangements. I tried to contact her throughout the day, but she didn't answer any of my calls. Later that afternoon, she drove up to our house in a red 2001 Mustang convertible. She was euphoric and wanted me to share her excitement of a lifelong dream come true.

I was skeptical because it was a used car and a convertible, and a Ford! There is a saying that Ford stands for "Found On the Road Dead." But Athena did not want to hear anything negative. Not then, and not when her dream vehicle gave her a multitude of problems. Especially when it rained. There was a gap between the convertible top and the car's body, and the seal had to be replaced several times. Even then, the problem didn't go away completely. On top of that, Athena financed the car through the Ford dealership, so the interest rate was in the stratosphere.

Figuring that if we were in a committed relationship, I needed to know her financial situation, I mustered the nerve to ask Athena for her credit report. Her reaction was like a volcano erupting. She was furious and showered me with several choice expletives. Then, she stormed out of the house and was gone for over an hour. When she returned, she was somewhat calmer. Undeterred, I requested her credit report again in the nicest possible manner.

To my surprise, she acquiesced, and we reviewed it together. Because I had recently eliminated my debt, I had some creds in that department. I told her about techniques for refinancing loans to lower interest rates, using the snowball technique to pay off credit cards—dealing with the biggest balances first and leveraging the momentum to pay off the smaller balances—and closing unused accounts. In retrospect, I can't imagine how terrifying it was for her to make herself vulnerable that way without us being officially engaged. Fortunately, we worked through it. She took some of my advice, and we emerged on the other side unscathed.

> **If you love someone, keep talking—nicely—
> until you find out what you need to know
> about each other.**

From August 2002 to June 2003, I had to report to Fort Lee, Virginia, for a Combined Logistics Captains Career Course (CLC3) in anticipation of a year-long tour in South Korea. By then, I knew Athena was the one. I proposed to her on December 27, 2002, in Tifton, Georgia, and she said Yes. That night, we set the wedding date for a year to the day later during my mid-tour leave from my Korean deployment.

$ $ $ $ $

Chapter 8

A$IAN DEPLOYMENT—
IN THE LAND
OF THE MORNING CALM

From June 2003 to June 2004, I was stationed in South Korea at Camp Carroll near the city of Waegwan in the area in the heart of the southern part of the peninsula. That area is very beautiful and amply justifies the descriptive phrase by which the entire nation is known. Its hills, mountains, and waters surround you with an atmosphere of peaceful tranquility, especially in the morning when the fog rises from the meadows covered with dew.

The Korean assignment was the best I had during my military career because of the place and the camaraderie among the service-members stationed there. I never had such intimate relationships on later assignments, and I am still in contact with several friends from that tour.

I also honed my leadership abilities and learned to be a staff officer. Although I was the junior ranking staff member, I led the biggest section—maintenance. I purchased several Korean furnishings, including a tapestry, a curio cabinet, a snow globe, figurines, and elephant sculptures, and had my wedding portrait painted.

Because I had plans to marry Athena halfway through my tour, I didn't want to live off base and immerse myself in Korean culture. I managed to cajole the housing staff into finding bachelor's officer quarters on base for me. It was a nice living arrangement, a second-floor apartment with two entries. My bedroom was on the front side facing the road, and in the rear was a sitting area from where I could view the newly built officer housing. I had a kitchenette with a refrigerator and stove, but I never used it, not even to boil water. I'm not much of a cook and don't have the patience to become one, although I have no problem waiting for a meal someone else prepares. One of my criteria for a serious girlfriend was her cooking skills. Athena can throw down in the kitchen, so I chose wisely.

The most important thing for me was to continue living debt free. I did not have a car loan to pay off because I'd totaled my 1994 Acura Legend in downtown Kansas City a month before I had to report to Korea. The vehicle was worth more than what I owed, so I received a $2,000 check from the insurance company, which put me on solid financial ground.

Because of my duty position as a maintenance control officer, the Army issued me a government phone for official business. I also had a pre-paid phone and put minutes on it to contact Athena and my family members. Since I had no exorbitant expenses, I set aside most of the money I earned to cover the cost of the wedding, started investing, and even had a few thousand dollars saved up that year.

I also contributed to the Thrift Savings Plan (TSP), a straightforward investment opportunity made available to all service members in 2003, regardless of duty station. Initially, TSP was a tax-deferred savings and investment plan for federal employees equivalent to corporate 401K for civilians. From the outset, I contributed 4% of my base pay which amounted to $155 a month.

I had planned to save money by eating at the mess hall on base, but our camp had the worst dining facility in the entire U.S. Army stationed in South Korea. I don't know what the problem was. The service staff and Korean nationals worked tirelessly to provide us with good food, but what they produced was all but inedible. The Thanksgiving and Christmas meals were the worst.

It got so bad that I would take the bus on Thursdays to another Army camp located in Daegu, about 40 miles to the north, to eat lunch there. Thursdays were soul food day, and the line of eager, hungry servicemen and women would wrap around the building. The kitchen made catfish, greens, ham hocks, Hoppin' John, macaroni and cheese, and a cornucopia of delicious desserts. I would invent meetings I had to attend at Daegu on Thursday to justify my presence there.

Do what is necessary to eat well!

The rest of the time, I went to an eatery on campgrounds, which had a sandwich shop, a pizza joint, a Burger King, and a booth with a Korean cook who served stir fry. That was tasty, but you had to get your plate before 11 a.m. because he stopped cooking at that point—what food remained would be on the line from then on until 9:00 p.m. Most days, Burger King was my go-to meal. I ate everything on the menu more times than I can count and cannot stand Whoppers and fish sandwiches to this day.

For recreation, we played flag football and held basketball tournaments. Besides sports, my favorite pastime was spending time in the Ville, a shopping and entertainment mecca outside the camp gates that catered to service personnel. You could find everything your heart desired there: clothes, shoes, boots, pirated movie DVDs, and more.

In those days, throwback jerseys and hip-hop gear, including Enyce and Rocawear, were popular. I bought all types of jackets, suits, and coats. I would send mink blankets and jerseys home upon request. I had my tuxedo made for the wedding there as well.

The strip clubs in the Ville were not really strip clubs or pleasure houses: there were no happy endings. Instead, "Juicy Girls" acted as hostesses. They didn't get that name because of looks or size. Upon entering a joint and getting seated, a young, scantily dressed woman in her late teens or early twenties—usually Filipino, Korean, and on occasion, Russian—would come to your table and take your order. She'd ask if you wanted company and would you buy her a drink? You'd get an alcoholic beverage while she would get non-alcoholic juice—hence the name "Juicy Girl."

If you weren't careful, you could get into serious trouble, especially if you started to take shots of Soju, a Korean vodka made from rice with 20% alcohol content. Your tab could end up in the hundreds of dollars, and you'd be out your entire pay. It happened all the time. Some service members got so involved they gave the Juicy Girl all their time and even proposed to their favorite. Unfortunately, the Juicy Girls had serious debts to pay off, and the GIs didn't have that kind of money. Also, the Juicy Girls were for everybody. (I am not saying that I was ever entertained by one. That's just what I heard! As an officer, I had to check out the places myself to see what my enlistees were up to!)

For my entertainment, I went to the on-base club, the Hideaway. I prided myself on drinking with the best of them and did my fair share of boozing, but I stayed away from Soju. That stuff would put you in the Matrix quickly. Fortunately, I did not have far to go after a night out when I had a few too many.

Besides the camaraderie, the best thing about the Hideaway was the late-night chicken wings and fries. Everybody tried to place a last order 30 minutes or so before the club closed.

Which brings me to an observation about black folks' behavior when it comes to money.

$ $ $ $

*The holy passion of friendship is so sweet
and steady and loyal and enduring in nature
that it will last through a lifetime,
if not asked to lend money.*

—Mark Twain

Chapter 9

CHICKEN WING DILEMMA AND FRIEND$HIP

When it comes to social get-togethers, I've noticed that black folks won't agree to pool money even when purchasing chicken wings. Now, who does not love an order of wings while watching sports or enjoying a gathering of friends? The dilemma occurs when there is a group of four or more, and someone suggests ordering chicken wings. Great idea! But...

There are choices to be made. Do we order from a chain restaurant or a local establishment? What flavors do we want: lemon pepper, Cajun, Parmesan, Hawaiian, or atomic hot, to name a few. Do we put more barbecue sauce on them or not? Decisions, decisions, but not insurmountable. So far, so good.

But when it comes to picking up the tab, determining who pays what amount can become a touchy issue.

In that regard, there are four different types:

- **The Sacrificial Lamb**
- **The Indifferent Man**
- **The Bill Guy**
- **The Imposter**

The Sacrificial Lamb willingly pays for the entire order. He's not necessarily interested in eating wings but enjoys the moment and company, so if an order of wings will keep the party going, he's all in.

The Indifferent Man does not mind contributing his fair share and happily provides whatever dollar amount the group agrees on.

The Bill Guy will contribute his portion once he looks the receipt over and does the math. He is only going to pay for the wings he ate. He always requests a separate check for dinner, although if somebody else agrees to pay the tab, he orders his fill.

Finally, **The Imposter**, who counts on other folks to pay, appears to be all in but has no plans to contribute because he'd rather use his money for his own stuff. However, he'll be the first to dig in when the wings arrive.

It may be different for women. Perhaps they are more selective in their company, hang out with like-minded friends, and adhere to the practice of "either we share or we pay on our own." Guys are focused on being around other guys regardless of their spending habits.

Myself, if a place is not too busy, I insist on individual checks, but if the joint is jumping, I try to streamline the payments to make it easy for the server. So, I usually end up being The Sacrificial Lamb because I believe life is short. No one knows the next time we will all get together, so I'll gladly pay for a good time. I prefer to surround myself with individuals who reciprocate or are at least willing to contribute. I pay for a round; you pay for the next round. Or, if you can't pay for the round, you'll cover the tip.

Be leery of the chicken wing dilemma. It can cause a lot of tension among friends. Try not to take the way others deal with the situation personally. It helps to remember that the behavior is about the individual's relationship with money, not necessarily how he feels about you.

> **Don't let the behavior of others
> get in the way of friendship.**
>
> **And don't be a moocher!**

$ $ $ $ $

Chapter 10

YOUNG LOVE AND WEDDED BLI$$ IN THE MILITARY

Athena and I got married in her hometown of Tifton, Georgia. The wedding ceremony took place at the Tifton Museum of Arts & Heritage. There were close to 200 attendees. The ceremony started on time, so if you were a couple of minutes late, you missed it. The moment that everyone remembers from both sides of the family is when one of Athena's aunts remarked, "you better treat her right because it's a whole lot of us." One of my first cousins retorted, "It might be a lot of y'all, but we bigger." Telling the story at family gatherings provokes laughter to this day.

The reception took place in a hotel banquet room. We paid for the maid of honor, bridesmaids, ushers, the best man's attire, the wedding and reception halls, and the food. We paid cash for everything, which raised some eyebrows. In those days, such financial transactions were handled by check or credit card.

The wedding was one of the finest moments of my life. Athena was gorgeous, and I could not believe how lucky I was that I was marrying her that day.

We didn't go on a honeymoon. I was not in the mood to travel, having to fly back to Korea to finish the second half of my tour. As a fellow officer, Athena understood. She returned to Washington, DC, to complete her training at Walter Reed Army Medical Center (now located in Bethesda, Maryland)

Because she wanted a career in the medical field, Athena hadn't been happy as a medical service officer. That position was more about leading and motivating troops than being hands-on. With her degree in Chemistry, she only missed one credit to meet the requirements to become a clinical laboratory officer. She enrolled in a biology course at Central Texas College and applied to the Army's Clinical Laboratory Officer Course in the summer of 2003. When she completed the program, she became a lab officer, making sure blood specimens were collected, properly stored, sent to the appropriate agency, and that results were provided in a timely manner. She worked closely with pathologists as well. Anytime that a soldier had any blood work done at a hospital, Athena would be in charge of ensuring everything went according to regulatory requirements.

It was an exciting time for her. In contrast, the rest of my tour in Korea was uneventful but seemed to take forever. I kept counting the days until it was over to go home and reunite with my wife. But upon my return to the States, Athena was stationed in San Antonio because of her new career path. I ended up in Washington State at Joint Base Lewis-McChord.

It wasn't until October 2004 that she was posted to Washington State and we lived under the same roof again—for the first time since 2002. We purchased a brand-new home in a new housing development near Olympia for $240,000. It was a two-story, four-bed, and 2.5-bath house. As a soldier or veteran, purchasing a home is not complicated. If you use your VA benefits, there are no down payments or closing costs. Everything is included in the loan. Our timing was good. The builder was struggling to meet demand, so prices kept rising. The same model we purchased in 2004 cost nearly $300,000 less than a year later.

On the Northwest Coast, air conditioning is optional, so we did not have it. Since it was just the two of us, we took our time furnishing the home, although we splurged on a bedroom set. As our first furniture purchase together, it felt special. Made of dark wood, it consisted of five pieces: the bed, a nightstand, a chest of drawers, and two small dressers. It has survived five moves, which included a cross-country shipment from Washington State to Virginia, and still looks good, even though we have not done anything special to preserve it, just dusting it now and then.

I also purchased a 2004 Suburban. I still own this car as well. Although it has 202,000 miles under the hood now, it is in excellent shape and going strong. I redid the upholstery a couple of years ago and plan to repaint it soon.

Financially, Athena and I were still on the same sheet of music. We did not use our credit cards and loan money or make any large purchases without consulting one another. At the time, I did not realize how much stress this put on her. Athena did not like having to check with me whenever she wanted to buy something other than everyday household items. I didn't think I was overbearing or over-controlling. I was doing what was best for us, although I never asked for her views. I thought she was all in, but that was not the case.

By October 2005, we had settled in, and things seemed to be going well. Athena was six months pregnant with our first daughter, and I was looking forward to becoming a father, although I didn't read or watch anything to prepare me. We selected the name when she conceived. I wanted the baby to have my initials C A L. Athena wanted to name her Chloe. I argued that Chloe sounded like chlorophyll which reminded me of plants. Athena agreed to the initials, and her sisters provided a list of names. We finally agreed on Chassidy.

Things were not great on the job for me, but I didn't dwell on it much. I should have been in the queue for a company command position because of my previous experience and military education. But I was newly assigned to the unit and, as an unproven officer, not considered for key jobs. Instead, I landed two lackey positions between two separate units with no responsibility or upward progress. The first was maintenance officer, but there was nothing to manage because most units were deployed. The other was rear detachment commander because the leaders wanted a Captain to sign for equipment, and I fit the bill.

$ $ $ $ $

Chapter 11

ANOTHER OVEREA DEPLOYMENT

One evening, just after Athena and I had finished dinner, my cell phone chimed. It was the Battalion Executive Officer. He informed me that I had been selected for deployment. That was all he knew. He could not tell me where I was going or for how long.

The news knocked the wind from me and sent my mind racing. Although I pulled myself together, in the back of my mind gnawed the fear that I would never see my unborn daughter. And that she would never see her daddy. However, over the next few days, I compartmentalized my thoughts and feelings to ensure that I was ready to perform my duties when the time arrived.

I was worried about Athena being alone, so I contacted her sister Lakesha and asked her to come and stay in our home in Washington State for a few months. As a newlywed mom with a toddler, she had stopped going to her local community college and didn't have a job yet to tie her down. So, she agreed and was there when Chassidy was born and lent a hand to Athena afterward. I'm glad she came. I'm not sure how things would have worked out without her help. It's great when friends and family members really support you.

The military does an excellent job of helping with your finances and other matters when they send you on a foreign mission.

They offered assistance in preparing a will and power of attorney free of charge. They set up allotments—automatic withdrawals from checking accounts where they wire your pay—to take care of mortgages, loans, life insurance premiums, money to family, and spousal support. They also provided me with a Service Members' Group Life Insurance policy for $400,000. I made sure all my financials were in order. Athena had access to all the accounts. Bills were paid automatically. For myself, during deployment, there was not much need for money because the Army took care of all my necessities.

After training at Fort Carson, Colorado, for 40 days, I deployed to Iraq in November 2005. I was on an eleven-man military transition team embedded with an Iraqi Battalion for mission support. Initially, we were based at Forward Operating Base (FOB) Warrior in Kirkuk, a city about 200 miles due north of Baghdad. After a couple of months, we relocated an Iraqi Battalion from there to East Samarra Airfield at FOB Mackenzie. Due to bureaucracy and ethnic differences, we never had our own life support contract to provide food, health care, waste removal, or fuel. We had to share with the Iraqis. Their leadership changed battalions every 30 days. The first group was very good, but the subsequent rotations were of a different caliber. The soldiers lacked discipline and often disobeyed orders. On one occasion, a few looted my team's food warehouse.

We went on daily patrols in armored truck convoys. We encountered sniper fire and improvised explosive devices (IEDs) designed to slow our movements and disrupt our mission to restore control of the area. Our machine gunner would return sniper fire from the turret of our armored Humvee and keep moving. IEDs were another story. Although we passed through the aftermath of several IEDs—a nightmarish landscape of burned-up vehicles, tires, busted glass, and strewn body parts in the black, ash-covered depressions created by the blast—we took a direct hit on only one occasion.

We were traveling in the desert in a three-vehicle convoy along the main supply route, and it was getting late toward the evening. I was the driver in the rear armored truck and the officer in charge that day. There were three other service members with me. The truck commander occupied the passenger side. The medic sat behind the driver's seat. The gunner handled the .50-caliber machine gun on the top of the vehicle. We had a Sudanese interpreter who spoke Arabic. He did not like the time of day we were returning to our FOB. He didn't say so directly but gave the impression that we would be attacked. He couldn't explain his feeling or where it might happen.

As we traveled, we noticed two Iraqi policemen by the road. There wasn't a checkpoint, so we did not stop. When my vehicle passed them, the other two trucks were 100 meters or so in front of me.

Suddenly there was an explosion as the IED hit the lead truck. It wasn't that loud, but I heard it and saw debris flying in the air. The truck commander next to me froze. He did not know what to do. As the rear armored vehicle, it was my job to block the road so no one could enter the area, and while I maneuvered the truck in place, the gunner was scanning the sector for a follow-up attack. My adrenaline was pumping, and I could hear my heartbeat hammering into my ears.

When the truck commander had processed that we'd been hit, he called for a status report from the soldiers in our lead vehicle via the radio. Fortunately, the IED was small and only blew out a tire and cracked the windshield. No one was injured, and there was no follow-up attack.

Our gunner was very angry. He believed the two Iraqi policemen planted the IEDs or knew who did. It was widely reported that the Iraqi police in the countryside were nothing but insurgents. He approached them locked and loaded. He had both of them get on their knees with their hands behind their head and began questioning them. He spoke a little Arabic. When he did not like their response, he slapped one in the back of the head. We pulled him off and calmed him down.

The Sudanese interpreter looked at me with an "I told you so" expression. I considered him honest and hard-working. He took the job to provide for his family. Perhaps he heard a prayer in Arabic that alerted him.

Before long, we were on our way again and made it safely to our FOB. There, repair crews replaced the windshield and tire. I reported to the base commander, relieved that no one was hurt because I had been in charge.

It may not seem like a big deal compared to what happened to others in my unit—some of them died in ambushes and mortar attacks—but my mind raced like crazy during the incident when I was trying to organize a response. The fear kicked in later on when I looked back and realized how lucky we were and how quickly things could have gone south.

The enemy would sometimes fire mortar rounds and send ground troops to finish the job. We provided security for the area and contacted an additional unit to ensure safe passage to the next FOB. My team returned to Kirkuk for the last two months of the deployment. My daughter, Chassidy, arrived while I was in Iraq. I was not there for her birth.

I thought a lot about never getting to meet her and her not getting to know me. Fortunately, I got a mid-tour furlough when she was three months old. I didn't know what it would be like to see her. But when I finally did, I kept being amazed and grateful that I had been a part of bringing another life into this world. I just wanted to hold her and take pictures when she was not sleeping. Seeing her made going back more difficult. However, back in the combat zone, I realized how fragile life is.

Many of my fellow service members sustained permanent injuries or paid the ultimate sacrifice of service to our country. I attended several memorials for fallen soldiers during my time in combat. At these ceremonies, I realized that these brothers in arms of mine were sons, brothers, uncles, husbands, and fathers. Sadly, some of them never got the opportunity to meet their children after they were born.

When I returned stateside for good in November 2006, Chassidy was nine months old. I expected some difficulty reentering normal married life but reconnecting with Athena turned out to be surprisingly easy. I was not overbearing and didn't feel I needed to establish myself as the "man of the house." I let Athena set the ground rules for parenting and followed her orders to the letter. The most challenging of her directives was to let Chassidy cry herself to sleep at bedtime. "Don't go in there for any reason," Athena insisted. It was tough, but I stayed the course. Taking Chaz to daycare and picking her up allowed me to get to know my daughter as Athena gradually integrated me into the daily activities. I returned to my usual chores: washing clothes, taking out the trash, doing yard maintenance, and washing our cars.

I was fortunate to return from the deployment unscathed. But being in a war zone really brought home that there is no guarantee you'll survive. The sense of one day you're here and the next you are gone struck me hard and changed my financial outlook. Until then, I was a penny pincher, turning over every dime before spending it. I only bought the things that we needed. I did not indulge in frivolous spending. But upon my return, I declared that life was to be lived and that I could not take my money with me when I was gone. Throwing caution to the wind, I went on a spending spree. I purchased a new car and a big flat-screen TV. If we were out shopping and Athena wanted something but thought it was too expensive, I put it in the shopping cart and proceeded to check out. I went down a financial rabbit hole and spent the next several years there.

As I think back, those were some great times, but I can't say I acted responsibly. Sometimes you can get caught up in having things, and your family is not your priority. My debt-free stint was only a year-long excursion, but I don't beat myself up over falling off the wagon. A challenging life event will always impact your finances. In my case, it was the deployment. As the saying goes, all gave some, but some gave all.

> **When faced with death,
> saving money becomes the least concern.**

$ $ $ $ $

Chapter 12

A LE$$ON
NOT LEARNED

We were doing well financially with two incomes and continued our spending spree. In anticipation of moving back east at some point, we bought a second house in Georgia. We figured we'd benefit from the increased home value of our Washington place. We projected that we'd make at least $50,000 from selling it.

But then, in 2008, the housing market crashed, home prices fell, and we were lucky to break even. In hindsight, it might have been better to hold onto the Washington house and rent it out, but I wonder if we could have carried three mortgages.

As it turned out, we relocated to Fort Belvoir in Northern Virginia. The houses there were very expensive, so we decided to rent. By then, we were expecting our second daughter, Camille. I was promoted to Major, so I had some additional money coming in.

I know now that you should invest or pay down bills when you have extra income. I did neither. I spent much of my free time at Potomac Mills, an outlet mall in Woodbridge, Virginia, and blew a lot of money there. Although we were doing OK financially, we could have done much better. I did try to refinance the second home, but because of the market crash, most banks required 20% cash to secure a loan. I could not use the VA loan program because it was not my primary residence. We still owed about $150,000 on that house, so we would have had to bring $30,000 to the table, and I was not interested in doing that.

$ $ $ $ $

Chapter 13

A MAN AND HI$ TRUCK

When I was still stationed near Tacoma, Washington, I purchased a 1977 Chevrolet C10 Bonanza. I'd been checking out the lemon lot at Joint Base Lewis-McChord. Where service members sold cars, boats, motorcycles, and other items they couldn't afford to take to their next assignment. I'd had my eye on the truck for some time. It was brown with tan in the middle of the side panels, a very popular color scheme for Chevy Trucks in the 1970s, and it had running boards on the side with two gas tanks.

Buying a thirty-year-old vehicle didn't make sense to Athena. We were selling our home and living in a Tacoma Travelodge, anticipating transitioning to a new assignment in the next two months. But after several discussions, she gave me the green light. I paid less than $3,000 for the truck—a steal even then.

I was super excited when I brought it home. One of Athena's friends was visiting and remarked, "What are you going to do with that big, nasty truck." That description stuck and became the truck's nickname, but I spelled it Big Nastee. It was my primary vehicle because I shipped the Suburban to the place of our next assignment. I loved driving it and basking in the admiring looks I got from people.

The month after I bought it, Big Nastee would not start. When I had it towed to the nearest service shop, Athena gave me a couple of uh-huhs, several side-eye jeers, and one I-told-you-so.

But replacing the ignition modulator cost only a couple of hundred dollars. Although the truck still had the original 305 motor, everything appeared to be in good working order.

But, one day, on my way to the Travelodge, Big Nastee did not respond when I pressed the gas pedal. I pulled over to the side of the road without incident and had it towed back to the service shop. The fuel pump had gone kaput and needed to be replaced to the tune of a few hundred dollars. I used the opportunity to update the tailpipes, an enhancement that gave them "elbows," and added Chevy tips to the end of the mufflers.

When it came time for us to move to Fort Belvoir in Northern Virginia, I paid to ship Big Nastee to Georgia, which cost me a cool $1,000. Athena considered Big Nastee a money pit, and she was probably right, but I already had plans to update my truck further.

Sometime after I got Big Nastee settled at our house in Tifton, I looked through my LMC catalog, which specializes in parts and accessories for Chevy and GMC trucks, imagining how dapper Big Nastee could look. I ordered replacement windows, outside mirrors, and other accessories. I had the windows tinted and sprayed the bedliner. I got a tag with Big Nastee inscribed and put it on the front bumper. Then, I bought some ten-inch subwoofers for the interior to play my music loud. I was going to get the truck painted, put some rims on it, and carry out whatever other crazy idea I could come up with.

> **The special love relationship between a man and his truck can really blind you to financial reality.**

At the time, Big Nastee was sitting in the driveway of our Tifton house collecting dust and pollen. It was 2009, and we were stationed at Fort Belvoir, Virginia, and there was nothing that required me to return to Georgia soon. But I kept fantasizing about finding some credible mechanic to do all the upgrades to my vehicle.

The following year, while I was deployed to Afghanistan, one of my brothers-in-law contacted me about using Big Nastee. Initially, I balked at his request, but when I thought about it, it didn't seem such a bad idea to let someone drive it instead of having it collect dust.

Big mistake!

It only took him a couple of months to blow the motor. There was nothing wrong with the engine. It was gross negligence on his part. I didn't get too emotional when I heard about it, though. I was in Afghanistan and had to maintain my focus on the mission. So, I instructed my brother-in-law to find someone to make the repairs.

Mistake number two!

I had extra funds from the deployment, so money was not an issue, although I should have been investing it or, better yet, paying down the mortgage on the Tifton home. But my ego was fixated on getting Big Nastee ready for some parking lot pimping when I returned—showing off my vehicle to gain attention and recognition.

My brother-in-law found some shade tree mechanics to do the repairs. They had an audio business and did not specialize in engine repair or replacement. I kept sending money to ensure things would get done promptly. After each payment, I asked my brother-in-law about the status. When he hemmed and hawed, I realized he was not being honest with me. I cursed him out and severed all ties with him.

By then, hundreds of my dollars had gone down the drain. The guy managing the repairs informed me that my brother-in-law had not paid all the bills. He'd skimmed a couple of hundred bucks at my expense. Mo money, Mo money.

Upon redeployment, I settled my charges. Big Nastee was not running well, but I ordered new rims and tires anyway. Another $1000 or so. At that point, I had no clue how much I had spent on Big Nastee. There's a saying: if you don't want to go deeper in the hole, stop digging. I was turning into a ditch digger.

As fate would have it, my next assignment was at Fort Benning, Georgia. One of my neighbors was a long-time friend from my Fort Hood days. He introduced me to his friend in Albany, Georgia, who ran a body shop and said he would paint Big Nastee and upgrade the motor as required. Finally, a professional, someone to make all my dreams come true and end the nightmare! So, I spent a few more thousand dollars on engine parts, paint job, and other miscellaneous items.

Again, I didn't keep track of the cost. If my wife had known how much I was shelling out, I would never have heard the end of it. By the time my tour of duty was closing out, Big Nastee was running well and looking good too. There was no need for parking lot pimping. I was turning heads in Albany as I traveled east on the South Georgia Parkway. Despite all the money I'd spent, I felt a sense of accomplishment. My bank account suggested otherwise.

Then the Army informed me that I had to report back to Joint Base Lewis-McChord in Washington State. Damn! I'd just spent all this money to upgrade my truck and couldn't enjoy it. There was no way I would take Big Nastee (or my Suburban) with me. When the mechanic who did the repairs suggested that he would maintain the vehicle while I was in Washington, I thought it was a win-win situation—I was concerned about theft and didn't want to leave my truck outside in the elements. The man had just painted it and done all the repairs. What better person to attend to Big Nastee in my absence?

Mistake number 3.

I was about to relive the same nightmare that I had with my brother-in-law. In hindsight, I should have parked Big Nastee in the garage and left the Suburban in the driveway.

Some months later, we flew from Washington to Georgia for a family visit during the holidays. I had some free time, so I stopped by the body shop in Albany to check on Big Nastee. I could not believe my eyes. My truck stood outside in the open air, surrounded by broken-down vehicles. It looked like it was in a junkyard. The owner tried to explain but coughed up nothing but excuses. I was livid and allowed it to ruin my holidays.

The only good thing that came from this ordeal was that the mechanic repainted the truck and made engine repairs at no cost to me. By then, I was tired of spending time, energy, and money on Big Nastee. I bought a truck cover, parked it in the driveway at our Tifton home, and called it a day. From 2015 on, Big Nastee was sidelined.

In 2018, my daughter Chaz asked if she could have Big Nastee. I had decided to retire from the military the following year, and her request inspired me—nothing like someone wanting something you've cast aside to reawaken your interest.

I wish I could say I had learned my lesson, but I continued my profligate spending, swapping out the motor, fixing an oil leak, and taking care of an issue with the rear main seal—mo money, mo money. But Big Nastee was roadworthy again.

I should be driving Big Nastee every day for the money spent, but I'm lucky if I put it on the road once a week. Reflecting on the initial purchase and the debacle with my brother-in-law, I realized it's always been about me. I was the common denominator in all the setbacks and foolish disasters. I could have told my brother-in-law, "Hell No!" I could have parked Big Nastee at my second home and put a truck cover over it. I could have purchased a crate motor and saved thousands of dollars. But I didn't.

I let my ego run wild and dug a deep financial hole.

$ $ $ $

Chapter 14

FOUR-WHEELER
IMPUL$E BUYING

Big Nastee wasn't the only extravagance I succumbed to during that time.

In 2008 on a family vacation in Tifton, en route to our duty station in Virginia, I was happy to reconnect with Big Nastee. At that time, it was parked at the house, and I drove it proudly through town.

Athena was six months pregnant with our second daughter, Camille. This would not be the best time to make any exuberant purchases. Unfortunately, when you're bored, it's hard to sit still, and what better way to enjoy life than spending money you shouldn't.

While Athena attended a Delta Sigma Theta (her college sorority) conference in Orlando, Florida, I went to the local motorcycle shop with my in-laws to window shop. Had my wife been with me, I wouldn't have gone inside. But a Four-Wheeler grabbed my attention. It was a yellow Can-Am, with space for hunting rifles/gear and a winch. Now, I am no hunter. I don't know how to employ a winch. Heck, I knew nothing about Four-Wheelers. But I had always wanted one.

That day, I used my better judgment and walked away, but I could not get the Four-Wheeler out of my mind. I felt I had to have it; more than that, I deserved it. Whatever hesitation I felt was banished by a voice in my head that said, "I can afford it!"

I discussed it with Athena that evening on the phone. She was exhausted from her conference. Tired of listening to me argue, she finally exclaimed, "Do what you want!" That was the green light for me. I went to the cycle shop the next day.

If you can't pay cash, it's probably a purchase you shouldn't make. Plus, I did not have a place to stay in Virginia yet, and no means to transport it even if I bought the Four-Wheeler. Yet, I was itching to buy it.

A friendly salesman named Bob greeted me; you know the type—who will not take no for an answer. The big yellow Four-Wheeler I wanted was unavailable, but Bob showed me a red Can-Am that looked the same but had no winch or a place for hunting gear. That eliminated two potential concerns. After he ran my credit report in his office and everything checked out, he offered to upgrade the rims and tires for a nominal fee. At that point, I was all in. I paid nearly $15,000 for the Four-Wheeler. For that price, I could have purchased two smaller ones, but I was enthralled and didn't think.

> **Unless you're Jeff Bezos or Elon Musk, and money doesn't matter to you, limit your budget for toys to $500.**

I didn't know how to get the gargantuan machine home, but the salesman assured me, "No worries, we will deliver it!" I felt like I was winning all around: getting what I wanted *and* the VIP treatment.

Then, the salesman asked, "What are you planning to use the Four-Wheeler for?"

I responded, "I'm not sure."

He suggested, "If you use it for farming, there are no taxes."

In my mind, I started singing "The Farmer in the Dell."

As promised, the dealership delivered my Four-Wheeler "Big Red" to our Tifton home, and I enjoyed riding it. My brothers-in-law did too, and everybody was having fun. Unfortunately, only one person could enjoy it at a time—two would have been better. But I didn't care. By then, my ego had swelled big enough to fill the entire house.

When Athena returned from her conference, to my surprise she liked Big Red, too.

About a week later, we had to depart for Virginia. I had no plans of taking the Four-Wheeler with me, but I was not dumb enough to leave it in the care of my brother-in-law. I had learned my lesson there. I took the key with me and parked the Four-Wheeler in the shed at the Tifton home. So, I had a big-ticket item to pay for while I was 700 miles away. Once again, I'd saddled myself with a big-ticket item that I couldn't use. My only financially smart move was that I paid off my luxury purchase in one year.

For the next three years, Big Red became a stationary shed dweller. In September of 2010, during rest and recuperation leave from Afghanistan, I discovered that it needed a new battery. Because I knew nothing about Four-Wheelers, let alone how to maintain one, I had not gotten a charger when I bought Big Red. As a result, my fun R&R activity consisted of having it towed to the repair shop, getting a new battery installed, and purchasing a charger as well.

Back in Afghanistan to finish my tour, on my weekly call with my wife, Athena informed me about a lawsuit. Remember when I became a farmer? Apparently, there were a lot of "farmers" like me who did not pay taxes at purchase. The IRS was foreclosing on that loophole and out to collect back taxes. I did not contest it. I knew I had tried to pull a fast one, and it had caught up with me, so I paid the taxes and penalty and moved on with my life.

I was fortunate to be stationed in Georgia from 2011 to 2013, so I would ride my Four-Wheeler at least once a month, but I had yet to get my money's worth out of it. Then, we had to move away again, and Big Red continued to sit in the shed. I could take solace in the fact that I owned it outright and that I was learning how to maintain it enough to keep it functioning.

In 2015, when we returned to Georgia, Big Red continued to shelter in the garage of our Tifton home because I had nightmares that someone would break into the shed. So, I insured the Four-Wheeler. When I let one of my sisters-in-law move into the house, I did not give her a key for Big Red.

As luck would have it, a few weeks later, I was visiting and figured I would take Big Red out for a spin. I tried to put the key in the ignition, but the ignition switch was gone. I was livid, but my sister-in-law gave me a blank look that, as far as I was concerned, spoke volumes. However, I had other priorities and did not get it fixed immediately.

Later, I figured I would repair it myself, so I went to a local dealership to purchase the part. That's when I learned that my current key would have to be updated with the new ignition switch. So much for being Mr. Fix-It! I decided not to use a local repair shop and brought Big Red to my current residence in Columbus, Georgia. A former colleague transported it for me. I waited a couple of months to get it repaired because I thought it would cost at least $1000. Fortunately, it turned out to be an inexpensive job.

On the other side of the coin, the Four-Wheeler is taking up space in my garage, and I don't live in a community where I can drive it around or go to mudding parks. I have owned Big Red for nearly 13 years, and it doesn't even have 300 miles on it. It's practically brand new. I contemplated selling it, but when I consulted Athena, she voted to keep it. I'm not exactly sure why. Perhaps she enjoys riding it and the fact that we own one. In any case, it means a lot coming from her. So, I will keep Big Red, like a trophy—great to look at, but to no practical purpose. I don't even like to tell folks that I own a Four-Wheeler because everybody asks where I ride. The honest answer is my garage, but I always provide a lame excuse.

Cars, trucks and other vehicles are obviously my Achilles heel. Confronted with a beautiful machine, all my good intentions for sound financial practice go flying out the window. I tell the cautionary tale of Big Nastee and Big Red at length not only to get it off my chest, but to let you know that I understand how difficult it can be to uproot deeply ingrained habits. As far as I'm concerned, Big Nastee and Big Red are family. At some point,

I will either sell or gift them to a family member because they deserve a good home.

> **If you can't get good mileage out of something you want, leave it in the store. Short of that: Have a big garage to park the toy you can't use.**

$ $ $ $ $

Chapter 15

CAMILLE
AND AFGHANI$TAN

My second daughter, Camille, was born in January of 2009. A month later, I was promoted to Major and graduated from Webster University with a Master's in Procurement and Acquisitions. For the next year, we settled into our new surroundings in Fort Belvoir, Virginia as a bigger family. Chaz was taking gymnastics and swimming lessons. Athena was nursing Camille and running the house. My grandmother, two aunts, and cousin lived nearby in Hampton, and we would visit them occasionally. It was good times that allowed us to bond as a family.

Then, in January 2010, I received deployment orders to Afghanistan. The Army only gave me seven days to settle my affairs before I had to report for training at Fort Benning, Georgia. Fortunately, when I talked with an empathetic assignment officer, he granted me a 30-day extension. Uncle Sam is the best, worst uncle one can have! Then, in February, a big snowstorm blanketed Northern Virginia, so I didn't ship out until March.

The military mandates that dual military couples and single parents establish a Family Care Plan so they can't use their children as a reason to avoid a deployment. So long as an area is safe, however, children can be assigned with their parents. But if it's a combat theater, kids are a no-go. I have witnessed dual military couples deploy at the same time to stay on the same cycle and leave the kids with other family members. Other couples have split those duties—one goes on combat duty, and the other stays home. We were fortunate that Athena had no operational or combat deployments after Kuwait. Because of her specialty as a laboratory officer, the military usually assigned her to bases with large medical centers. While she had to be available for overseas service, it wasn't likely to happen. As a result, she could be a full-time mom for our daughters.

My time in Afghanistan was nothing like my Iraq deployment. For the Middle East assignment, I trained for more than thirty days before departing; for Afghanistan, only a week. Because it was so brief, I assumed the mission would be less kinetic, meaning we would not spend as much time outside the safety of our compound. Upon arrival at Camp Eggers in Kabul, I realized I was right—the job would be more administrative than tactical.

In Iraq, it was not a matter of if we were going to be hit by enemy fire, but when. In Afghanistan, there was a good chance we would finish our tour unscathed. During my Iraq deployment, I was heavily armed, and we drove around in armored Humvees with machine guns mounted on the roof. Every driver and passenger had a rifle. I even possessed a few hand grenades. In Afghanistan, I carried a 9mm pistol and borrowed an M16/M4 rifle for additional fire power when I had to leave the camp. Our vehicles were armored SUVs, and the rules of engagement did not allow us to leave them for any reason. That was tough for me because, in Iraq, the battle drill was to protect everyone at all costs. If we needed to dismount our vehicles, we did. But in Afghanistan, our orders were: do not break the seal of the vehicle, to stay put and call for reinforcements. Fortunately, I did not have to leave the camp very often, and was never shot at or encountered an IED.

The location in the country's capital was strategic, and our activities ran more to advisory than to direct participation in combat operations. Our mission was to build up the Afghanistan National Security Forces (ANSF), advise, and ensure that they took the lead on operations. We were not conducting daily patrols to engage and defeat the Taliban, who had retreated to the countryside. There was some "green on blue" violence when ANSF—green—would assault or kill a representative of the International Security Assistance Forces (ISAF)—blue—which included the U.S. military. It didn't happen very often, but it was a big deal when it happened and made everyone nervous.

Camp Eggers had troops from several countries: Albania, Australia, England, France, Germany, Italy, Mongolia, Poland, Romania, and Turkey. I loved interacting with enlisted soldiers and officers from other countries and learning their languages, traditions, and values. I pride myself on being a man of my word no matter what continent or country and regardless of cultural differences. I found that like-minded people recognize that quality in one another and appreciate it. I'm still in contact with several friends I made during that time.

Before I went to Afghanistan, I created a Facebook page so Athena, my daughters, and I could have an additional way to communicate besides phone calls and postcards. During that time, I started to lift weights and met good people, including a few female service members. The pictures I posted looked like we were on vacation and not in a combat zone.

However, I wasn't happy that the deployment impacted my professional timeline and set me back a year. By the time I finished the tour, most of my peers had completed their educational requirements for the rank of Major, and I had not. I was concerned about being competitive for the next rank. I planned what to do during the deployment if I did not receive a promotion. I reviewed my finances and decided that I had three years to become debt free. However, I decided to make career decisions based on what was best for my family and ignore the career progression requirements.

When I rejoined my state-side Army organization, it was in the process of relocating, so everything was in flux. I didn't have an assigned position, and no one knew who I was because my former coworkers had moved on. The military doesn't concern itself much with the psychic well-being of its soldiers. It expects them to cope on their own. But uncertainty at work can cause a lot of additional anxiety and make it harder for a family to deal with issues of its own.

My biggest mistake was not treating Athena as a priority. I didn't consider that she had both girls while working and attending school. I was selfish. It was all about me. So, when I returned home in March 2011, she was not thrilled to see me. Chaz was ecstatic. Camille, a toddler now, followed her sister's lead, but I was still a stranger to her. It took a few years before I was fully integrated into my family again.

$$ \$ \$ \$ \$ \$ $$

Chapter 16

FINANCIAL $HUTTLE

In July 2011, we relocated from Fort Belvoir, Virginia, to Fort Benning, Georgia, for our next assignment. Chaz was starting kindergarten, and Camille was going to daycare. Athena was uncomfortable with the local community schools and wanted to live on base. She consulted with some of her peers, and they endorsed on-base housing. Unfortunately, the accommodations were not big enough for all our furniture, so we donated some to one of Athena's sisters. It didn't matter to me. I adhered to the motto "Happy wife, happy life."

The U. S. military provides a Basic Allowance for Housing (BAH), which is nontaxable. When you live on base for free, the military retains the entire housing allowance. This isn't always a good deal. Say, my allowance is $1800, the Army keeps the whole amount. However, if I were renting/purchasing off base for $1,600, I would keep the $200 difference. As the marching cadence goes, "They say that in the Army the pay is mighty fine, they give you hundred dollars and take back ninety-nine, oh lord I want to go!"

On the other hand, being on base had some benefits, including lower prices when shopping at a commissary, a post exchange, and cheaper gasoline. Of course, every soldier has the privilege of shopping there, but not needing to leave the base most of the time is convenient.

I was less pleased with the cost of daycare. Camille spent the entire day there, and Chaz went before and after school. The fees were based on our ranks. Athena and I were Majors at the time, so we paid more than many other parents. My running joke was: I am spending all this extra money, but my kids are using the same bathrooms and drinking the same water as the other kids. There were no special diapers provided. My kids did not get credit for vacation time, so I still had to pay to maintain their slot even when we were out of town.

The tour at Fort Benning was cut short a few months before my two-year requirement. I was the Battalion Executive Officer, and the Battalion Commander I served was being replaced. There was no incentive for me to work with the incoming Commander, so I used some of my vacation days to leave my position early. I had nearly 90 vacation days on the books and took about 60 days of "transitional leave." Normally, per Army regulations, I would have been authorized to only take up to 30 days of leave. But because I was changing duty stations, what is known as Permanent Change of Station (PCS) leave, the 30-day requirement did not apply to my situation. Thus, I was able to take more time off.

I was tired of losing my BAH and paying a mortgage as well as childcare costs. Then I had a crazy idea and pitched it to Athena: we would live in our house in Tifton and commute to Fort Benning, a 125-mile one-way drive. That would allow me to retain my BAH money to cover our mortgage. And we only had to do it for a month and a half until we'd be relocated to Washington State for our next assignment. Athena agreed to the plan so long as I did all the driving.

This was our daily routine. We would wake up Chaz and Camille about 3:30 a.m. and start out no later than 4. We drove in our 2007 Chrysler 300 with HEMI via Highway 82, a multi-lane thoroughfare. There were only a handful of small towns to travel through where we had to slow down—Sylvester, Albany, and Dawson. When we got to Ft. Benning, I dropped the girls off at the childcare center, and took Athena to work at the hospital. Then I headed to my former office or the library to complete a distance learning course for the Army. Around 4:30 in the afternoon, I collected the girls, picked up Athena and drove back to Tifton. Fortunately, Chaz and Camille were too young to make sense of their dad's madness. There were no complaints of, "Are we there yet? They slept going and coming.

Most people might think the money wasn't worth the time spent on the road. All in all, we probably saved less than $5,000. But Athena and I had some of our best conversations traveling back and forth. Plus, we spent time in our home in familiar surroundings. The memories were worth ten times more than any minutes spent in the car.

> **Saving money is always good, but the bottom line isn't always the most important thing.**

It might have been different if we had some mechanical issues. But the universe was on our side: there were no accidents or breakdowns. Sometimes I zipped along way past the speed limit, I never got a ticket. Sometimes a crazy idea is worth it in ways you never imagined. Sometimes the Law of Unintended Consequences works to your benefit.

We hold these truths to be self-evident, that all men
are created equal, that they are endowed by
their Creator with certain unalienable Rights,
that among these are Life, Liberty and…

— The Declaration of Independence

Chapter 17

THE PUR$UIT OF PROPERTY

In 2011, we relocated from Fort Belvoir, Virginia, to Fort Benning, Georgia. During the transition, we visited with family in Tifton. My father-in-law took me on a ride-along to look at his properties. At the time, he owned ten single-family homes. I wondered how much money he earned and asked how he acquired them. For him, it was easy. He was well known and respected in town, so when someone wanted to sell their home, he got first dibs. He purchased properties for $10,000 to $15,000, fixed them up, and rented them out.

It occurred to me that Athena and I could do that too. But when I suggested that we buy another property in Tifton as well, she was reluctant at first. She questioned how would we secure the money for the purchase. Because of the 2008 housing market collapse, we had no equity in our Tifton summer home. Having barely broken even from the sale of our house in Washington State, we didn't have much savings either. I didn't know it then, but I could have borrowed against my Thrift Savings Plan. Still, we owned a 2004 Suburban and a 2007 Chrysler 300, and I borrowed against both cars to obtain $25,000.00 in seed money. Cash in hand, Athena and I searched until we found a property that met our financial threshold, a 4-bed, 2-bath home in foreclosure.

The realtor who helped us buy it for $22,000 asked an important question, "What are you going to do with the property?"

We responded like babes in the woods, "We don't know."

He exclaimed, "You are wasting money if you don't act right away so it can provide you with income."

That was my first lesson in real estate acquisition.

Then, we got lucky.

The house was in poor condition, but the home inspector gave us the name of a contractor. We put all our trust in a stranger, but he was the real deal. I had to pay him weekly, but the house was ready in 30 days and rented immediately. We used Lowe's and personal credit cards and cashed out a mutual fund to finance the rehab. As it turned out, we spent more fixing up the place than we did buying it, but it didn't matter. We were in the game.

Immediately, we experienced the good, bad and ugly aspects of becoming landlords.

- The good: the property was now in excellent condition.

- The bad: frequent tenant turnover—we had three different renters in two years.

- The ugly: exterminating bed bugs, cutting down trees, and repairing broken sewer lines.

We managed the property ourselves for a couple of years, but being out-of-state landlords proved too difficult and exhausting. We finally heeded the advice of others and hired a property manager. Had we known the benefits—he found a tenant that we've had for more than seven years—we would have switched over earlier.

In 2018, we purchased two duplexes in Ashburn, Georgia, owned by Athena's brother. He needed cash, and we didn't haggle over the price. Ashburn has only 4,000 inhabitants, but several industrial plants are nearby, so new people coming to town are always looking for a place to live. Both properties were dilapidated. The roofs needed replacing. The bathrooms and kitchen were outdated. A couple of the apartments had no flooring, only the concrete slab on which the house was built. When I told Athena that I was not interested in being nobody's slum lord, we had to fix them up right. She gave me her full support.

We turned the properties over to our property manager. Three of the tenants decided to renew their leases. The fourth refused to comply and abandoned his apartment. It was in the worse shape of all. It was my first rehab as a foreman, and I wanted to whip the property into shape quickly, but I underestimated the time it would take. I failed to account for windows that needed to be special ordered, which added four weeks to my timeline. The roofing contractor required 30 days before he could start the job. I was already off to a poor start. It was a good thing that I could laugh at myself. I'd figured my money and energy would be enough, like waving a magic wand and voila! Everything would come together as I wished. When that didn't happen, I maintained a glass-half-full approach, however, and started cleaning up the mess around the property, making several trips to the landfill in the next county. These trips were unnecessary because the city serviced the rubbish. I could have saved time and money if I had known the waste management procedures.

Because I didn't know any contractors in the area, I used five different contractors. That wasn't the best approach by any means, but if necessity is the mother of invention, it's also the father of cooperation, and we were cooperating like never before. One guy updated the electrical and plumbing. He was no perfectionist, but he accepted moonshine for payment. He was eager and easy to find as long as I had some on me. I kept plenty of jars of shine during this time. The local heating/AC company installed central air and heat. Someone from the next county installed the windows. He didn't have transportation and needed money up front to secure his business. I gave him what he needed, and he did an excellent job. I asked one of my first cousins from South Carolina to help with painting, demolition, and door installation. He did a lot of heavy lifting. Without him, it would have taken much longer to renovate the apartment.

After several trips to the landfill, I had a fortuitous encounter. I stopped at a local store in Arabi, Georgia, for a beer during my final run to the dump on a long day. As I approached the counter, I noticed several business cards, and one was for a contractor named Richard Butler. I grabbed one and telephoned him right away when I made it back to the rental property. He came over within the hour. By this time, the apartment was gutted to the studs. You could see through the kitchen to the bathroom. We conducted a walk-through. As this was my first rodeo, I was pleased when Richard asked questions about things I had not considered and went along with his recommendations.

I stopped calculating the amount of money I had already expended and asked him for an estimate of what it would take to complete the job.

When Richard told me, I asked, "How do you take payments, and when?"

He smiled. "I don't take any money until the job is complete."

Hallelujah!

That's what I said to myself. I responded, "You are hired."

I did not bother to contact anyone else. Most people believe it's foolish not to request additional quotes, but it's hard to find honorable, professional people who know what they're doing in this business. Sometimes, it is better to be lucky than good.

Richard did a great job finishing the project and works with me to this day. I have called on him for countless jobs. No job is too big or too small. He always works me into his schedule and charges reasonable rates. He does not require supervision. If something is not right, he'll call me. I leave him the key and get out of the way. Most time, we don't even write up a contract, just a good old southern handshake.

The apartment was ready for rent in November 2018. The lessons from that first experience have become part of my DNA. I learned that you could save a lot of money if you do the demolition and clean up yourself. That allows the contractor to come in and get right to work. Most importantly, there's no certification required or special skill set to break stuff. However, when it comes to tearing up sheetrock and removing plumbing, flooring, and busted doors, I am something of an expert.

The duplexes were running efficiently with no major repairs or tenant turnover. During COVID-19, every tenant paid without any issues. But in November 2022, we had to evict two tenants for being in arrears. Fortunately, the evictions were drama free. However, one of the tenants, an aspiring R&B artist, built a studio inside one of the bedrooms so he could record music. It was a sturdy structure with two-by-fours, sheetrock, and noise-canceling foam, and taking it down was a nuisance. I had to remove several different types of screws and nails and, when all else failed, took a sledgehammer to it to vent my frustrations.

> **Always have a sledgehammer handy for demolition.**

In 2021, Athena and I acquired two additional properties via a tax sales auction. Both were severely distressed and would be better razed than rehabbed. Still, they belong to us because we have been paying the taxes. One of the properties has sentimental value because it was Athena's great-grandmother's residence. My wife was very proud when she outbid the other participants. However, it will take more than pride to resurrect this home. It will take cold hard cash and some gymnastics with other assets.

That leads me to another lesson: don't out-leverage yourself. The market will fluctuate, and you can exploit it with cash on hand. On the other hand, having too much debt during a down market could lead to your premature exit from the real estate game. In this instance, I have two lessons in conflict with each other. It would be best if you rehabbed these properties as soon as possible because you're losing money. The other side of the coin is the potential to overextend credit with no positive cash flow. There are no right or wrong choices, only good moves.

Our goal is two-fold: provide quality and safe living for our tenants and give us an income stream. Our strategy is small-town deals only. I realized there are lucrative opportunities nationwide, but I don't want to take on the hassles of a large-scale geographic approach. The funny thing about the small-town approach is that everybody knows who you are, which has pros and cons. I don't have an issue with a tenant contacting me directly about issues despite having a property manager: just a way, not *the* way. We use a property manager to maintain distance between the tenants and us. The pros are knowing the temperament of the local population and the busybodies that keep us informed on goings on with the properties.

The girls' activities preclude us from spending much time at our summer home in Tifton. Currently, it sits vacant but is well maintained and is a potential income source. Athena and I are considering converting it into an Airbnb or short-term rental. There is nothing like an asset that can pay for itself.

The rental properties are a critical but complex portion of our financial portfolio. They provide cash flow and a hedge against inflation. On the other hand, it's not easy to liquidate them for quick cash, and they can't be sold without a substantial tax bill. The properties resemble mutual funds because there could be significant financial gains over a 10- to 20-year span.

But as a family legacy, my daughters are not interested in any of the properties at this stage. They can't understand why we continue to purchase such eye sores. During the past Christmas holidays, Athena paid them to clean one of the apartments. The lesson of generational wealth was lost on them, but the opportunity to earn spending money was motivation enough.

I want these properties to become generational wealth for my daughters, but the reality for now, it's just my hobby. My girls don't view what I do as a job. Maybe, when I don't buy them their heart desires, I'll blame it on the lack of money from the rental properties.

I have some advice for anyone wanting to get into the real estate game.:

- Be patient. Not everything can be done as a quick fix.
- Be creative when finding money.
- Build a team of contractors, suppliers, and managers. That's how you will make things happen unless you do all the work yourself.
- Be prepared to get dirty.
- Sometimes it's about saving money, and sometimes it's understanding what the real problem is.

Above all, be humane and stand for something. As a landlord, I don't care about anyone's ethnic background or socioeconomic status. What matters is that people are decent and responsible. Since reading the book *Evicted: Poverty and Profit in the American City* by Matthew Desmond, I have made it my vow not to become a slum lord, regardless of what it may cost me in money. My reputation matters more to me than ignoring a tenant with an issue. I live in a good home, and I want my tenants to be proud to invite folks over and not have to run the faucet to flush the toilet.

$ $ $ $ $

Chapter 18

CARING FOR
FAMILY MEMBER$

In 2012, my mom, living in our childhood home in Mississippi, had a serious fall. She couldn't get up on her own, and nobody knew how long she lay helplessly on the living room floor before a neighbor found her. Fortunately, she didn't break any bones and was OK, but her accident became a wake-up call for my brother and me. We decided that she could no longer live alone. My brother did not have enough space at his house to take her in. I was still serving in the military, and our family's living quarters were not an option either. So, we decided to relocate her to Walterboro, South Carolina, where she grew up. Her sisters lived there, several relatives and friends. It seemed like a good solution, and my brother and I acted unilaterally: We took zero input from our mom. When she asked where she would go, I told her I would find a house.

My dad always conducted the financial business for the family, as was usual for married couples of his generation. He wrote the checks. He balanced the accounts. He took out loans and obtained credit cards. My mom just went along for the ride. When they divorced in 2001, she received the house, a car, and a portion of his 401K.

I never concerned myself with her finances. I didn't review the divorce decree or step in to assist her. I was living with my kids and Athena and figured Mom was doing OK. But after the accident, I looked at her money situation and quickly realized that she had made poor financial decisions. Because she didn't know anything about mutual funds, individual retirement accounts, or investments, she just spent the money from the 401K plan and had nothing to show for her efforts.

> **While caring for someone, it's essential to know all the facts about their money and actively participate in any financial decisions.**

I sprang into action in my usual no-holds-barred fashion and found a place for her in Walterboro, an "as is" purchase. It was a brick house with three bedrooms, two bathrooms, and hardwood flooring throughout, large enough to have someone live with her comfortably.

After the housing bubble burst, I had a hard time securing a mortgage. It was no longer 2007 when banks were handing out loans like candy. At the time, I was living on base at Fort Benning, Georgia, and owned our summer home in Tifton. Because I had no other assets, no mortgage lender would give me money at a favorable rate.

The house cost $58,000, and I managed to secure a 30-year mortgage with a 20% downpayment and a balloon payment at the end. Add to that the expenses to make the place livable, and I was $30,000 in cash out of pocket.

The monthly payment for the mortgage was $664.00. I figured that the $500 from Mom's social security and the $300 a month I received from the rental of our childhood home would cover most of the living costs, including utility bills and any maintenance issues, but they did not. Initially, my brother received my mom's social security check at his address. He also collected the rent, but he was never consistent with remitting the funds to me. Sometimes it took him a couple of weeks after the first of the month, and I had to use some of my money.

We bought the house in October, and my mom moved in by the end of the year. My brother and I made a sound decision for her, and I felt good about it, even if I had to shoulder the financial burden.

Her initial housemates were one of my first cousins and her son. My brother and I did not ask her to contribute to the rent or the utility bills. I took care of the mortgage. My brother paid the water, electricity, cable, phone, and internet bills with Mom's social security money. I did not trouble myself with those bills because I wanted my brother to participate in caring for our mom.

All the bases seemed covered, but the honeymoon didn't last long. We failed to convey our expectations to our cousin to help care for our mom because we thought it was implicit in the arrangement. My brother and I thought our cousin had the deal of a lifetime, but she felt she had her own life to live.

**When money is in play,
it is prudent to have a contract,
especially if it involves a family member.**

As time passed, my brother did not trouble himself with the business any further, but I spoke to my mom often and did not like what I was hearing. I voiced my concerns to my cousin and aunt, but to no avail. By the time a year had passed with no improvement, I had decided that my cousin had to go. She left without complaint.

But when we had another cousin and her two kids move into the house in Walterboro, things went from bad to worse. Not only did she ignore my mom more than her predecessor. Everything seemed to break after she arrived. During the summer, the air condition-er malfunctioned. By then, I was stationed in Columbus, Georgia, and I told my cousin to have someone fix it. Instead of contacting a repairman, she bought herself an A/C window unit for her room. What really ticked me off was that other family members who lived nearby knew that the air conditioner was on the fritz, but no one tried to assist my mom or me. I had to contact a repair outfit myself and explain the circumstances to remedy the situation.

When I expressed my discontentment to my aunt, who is my mom's younger sister, about how her daughter treated my mom, she did not take me seriously. That irritated me to no end. It be-came emotionally draining because my mom called every other day with another issue. Again, my brother did not concern himself with any of it. He left me to deal with it and call all the shots.

I made up my mind that Mom would come to live with me and discussed the situation with Athena. She agreed it was the best course of action, and we mapped out a plan. It would be finan-cially challenging, but at least it would end all the bickering and frustration of trying to help my mom from a distance.

Thus, commenced what I named Operation Fury—relocating Mom and dealing with her house in South Carolina. She was al-ready spending the Christmas holidays with us, so we set D-Day for the rest of the move on January 1, 2017.

I left South Georgia for Walterboro early on New Year's Day. Upon arrival, I started cleaning the house and determining what to keep and what had to go. I loaded up my truck and took it to the Colleton County dump the next morning, only to find out that it was still closed for the holidays. Damn. I had a fully loaded vehicle with no place to dispose of all the unwanted stuff and no plan B. Fortunately, when I called around, one of my cousins told me about another dump just up Highway 15 in St. George, which was open. It was about 30 miles away, and I made four trips there that day, discarding an old bed, dressers, lamps, and trash.

I also made three trips to Goodwill to donate a recliner, a sofa, and a television because they were fairly new items. I kept the brand-new TV, washer, dryer, and bed frame. I did all the lifting and hauling by myself. (I have a bad habit of not asking for help because I figure people complain too much and will let me down. I know that I can count on me, myself, and I.)

When I was finished, I met with the realtor. She introduced me to a handyman who would take care of the lawn maintenance and do minor repairs. I told her she was welcome to take anything left in the house and headed back to Tifton.

On the way home, I reflected how people come out of the woodwork when you pack up a place. Members of my family and neighbors called me throughout my stay, asking about what I was going to do with various items. They were surprisingly well-informed about the contents of my mom's house. They were also eager to know if I would keep and rent the home. Where had they been when my mom needed their help? I wanted to put this emotional and financial fiasco behind me and was in no mood to talk, so I was rather terse with them. That created a narrative in my extended family that has lasted to this day about how badly I had treated my cousins and how stingy I was with my relatives, but I don't care.

As I mentioned earlier, I paid the house off within three years of buying it. But it took about nine months to sell after my mom moved in with me. Because it was not my primary residence, the government took 28% of the proceeds. I could have filed paperwork to reduce the tax cost, but that would have required purchasing another property, and I wasn't interested in doing that. So, I just took the hit. Athena was unhappy with me and remained annoyed about my lackadaisical financial attitude for several months.

She also kept badgering me to change the arrangement with my brother so my mom's social security check would come directly to me. I didn't want to deal with it because I did not want to appear greedy. Friends told me several horror stories about siblings quarreling over their parents' finances. But Athena persisted until I talked with my brother. I anticipated it would be a difficult conversation, but to my surprise, he didn't question my motives and readily agreed. I owe a lot to Athena for pushing me. Had she not insisted, I would have just maintained the status quo and driven myself crazy about what my brother was doing with the money.

When I took Mom to the local social security office to update her address, the employees looked at me like I was a mugger trying to steal from an older person. When it comes to taking care of elderly folks, everybody thinks you're ready to mooch off their social security benefits, disability payments, pension, and other retirement funds. Don't pay them any mind. They do not matter. What is imperative is that you get access to all financial accounts of your parents or relatives that require assistance—all bills, insurance, mortgage, investments, taxes, car loans, etc.

In 2017, my mom's benefits amounted to $1551 a month— not a lot to live off, just enough to scrape by. I planned to save her money because I could pay for everything she needed with my income. That way, her benefits could contribute to a fund for her three grandchildren—my daughters and my brother's son. I felt that our kids should have money available to finance their college education, buy a home, or start a business. I do the same with the rental proceeds from my childhood home for Chaz and Camille. So, I made the unilateral decision to invest my mom's social security benefits. I feel it was the right choice. Sometimes, though, I wish I weren't the only one looking out for the future and thinking about family legacy.

> **If you are the primary caregiver for someone, it's nobody else's business what you do with their money.**

Although I admit, I still wrestle with how my mom's money is invested and used because I want to be transparent and honest about what I do for her with my extended family.

As of this writing, my mom continues to live with us. At age 72, she is not in the best shape. Since 2017, she has fallen several times, and she requires a lot of daily care, from making sure she eats, keeping her medications current, and maintaining her schedule of doctors' appointments.

I have to do most of my personal activities early in the morning or late at night when she is in bed. But there is no way I could allow my mom to live in a less desirable place when I know I can do better for her. It is like when I was in the military: She is a mission, and the mission cannot fail. So, I do what must be done.

$ $ $ $

Never say you know a man until you have divided an inheritance with him.

—Johann Kaspar Lavater

Chapter 19

LIFE IN$URANCE, BURIAL$, AND WILL$

That brings me to life insurance. Since we, as a nation cannot agree on universal health care, one can only imagine folks' various takes on life insurance.

When I grew up, folks used to go around with blinders and didn't bother to obtain a policy. I have never been big on empirical evidence, but I imagine your average Black person does not care much for life insurance.

There are historical reasons for that. Traditionally, life insurance was marketed to Black Americans as burial insurance. After the Civil War, insurers began classifying Black people who were former slaves as having higher mortality risks and charged them more premiums than white people or denied them coverage altogether. The practice extended into the 1960s. Although some states outlawed race-based underwriting, many insurance companies left and took their racist practices elsewhere. They also found creative ways not to pay claims. No wonder Black people distrusted insurance companies then and continue to be suspicious now.

That seems to be changing. According to a 2021 Barometer Study, 56% of Black Americans purchased policies that year, the highest rate among all racial groups. I consider that a good thing because, unless you come from wealth, it is difficult to acquire any assets or leave a legacy without a life insurance policy. After all, most people make just enough money to cover household expenses. Many don't own homes, and those who do are often cash-poor because they constantly tap into their equity to consolidate debt or finance a child's education.

Yet, life insurance is the one monetary instrument that can really improve a family's financial situation. Depending on the size of the policy, the money can pay off the family home, fund education, or go toward investments. And, it's relatively inexpensive compared to car and mortgage payments.

There are three types of life insurance

- Term
- Whole
- Universal

Term life insurance is the least expensive, although it only covers the insured for a designated time period. But it can be converted into a whole life policy. A whole life policy covers insureds over their entire life span, and the premiums are fixed. A universal policy covers insureds as long as the premiums are paid, but they can increase. If an employer offers insurance coverage, that's an optimal way to obtain low-cost coverage.

Both whole life and universal policies pay out dollar amounts at termination. The whole life payout is fixed, whereas a universal policy payout is subject to change. For example, a universal policy may have a face amount of $100,000. Due to how long one has owned the policy and various associated fees, the beneficiary may receive only $90,000.

I owe my outlook on insurance to my time in the military. The Army makes it easy to get through Service Members' Group

Life Insurance (SGLI), which provides $400,000 coverage for a premium of $24 a month. I signed up as soon as I was commissioned and participated in SGLI for the duration of my military service. Athena did too. After retirement, I acquired a 30-year term life insurance policy to ensure my family is taken care of financially when I meet my maker.

> **A life insurance policy is a must
> if you are serious about creating generational wealth.**

Still, I understand that getting life insurance may be difficult, but people should at least have a plan to cover their funeral arrangements. Death is a certainty for everyone, and there are too many stories of black folks who don't have enough money to bury their loved ones. That, in turn, leads to the circulation of the collection plate at church and the creation of Go Fund Me accounts to solicit the necessary funds.

I am always amazed at the amount of food at people's funerals. There may not be enough money to bury the person, but there is plenty for food and all the to-go plates that people pack up as they depart the event.

So, it is prudent to plan for one's death and, at a minimum, obtain a burial insurance policy from a funeral home. As I am writing this, the cost ranges from $28 to $116 a month and covers burial expenses not exceeding $10,000.

One alternative to reduce the funeral costs of a full burial is cremation. But that is virtually taboo in the black community. We must see the body go into the ground. Anytime I have a conversation with family members about death and mention the word cremation as a viable option, I'm met with universal jeers and frowns. No one ever counters with logic or reasoned arguments.

The conversation usually ends with, "We don't believe in cremation."

I usually try to get in a dig like, "What will it matter."

And I get the same response, "We don't believe in cremation, next subject."

That brings me to the subject of making a will. There is nothing worse than a family fighting over the house and other valuables their loved one left behind—everybody quarreling about what they were promised or owed to them. Unresolved issues with the deceased rear their heads and become heated arguments over money and who deserves what.

I know of a family in which the mother won the lottery to the tune of several million dollars. When she died soon after without a will, her three grown children (in their 40s and 50s) disagreed on how the money should be divided. They sued each other and the lawyers ended up getting most of the winnings. The children all ended up with less money than they would have gotten if they'd just settled without litigation.

A will won't automatically guard against emotional outbursts and disputes. It isn't a panacea. It won't stop survivors from getting sore at each other. But it doesn't hurt to have one because it provides a legal means to adjudicate financial disagreements. Emotions may still run high, but the will establishes and codifies the private conversations family members might have had and sets forth how property and money will be distributed.

Of course, a will can be contested, but seeing the deceased's wishes written in black and white usually is enough of a dose of reality. Besides, most people who fight over money don't have the financial wherewithal to contest a will anyway. Those who do often spend more money on attorneys than they would get if they just sat tight and accepted reality.

If you don't want to get a will, you should at least put the name of another responsible family member on your deeds and bank accounts. Also, update your beneficiaries on your life insurance policies and retirement plans. Ideally, keep a record in one place of your policies, car papers, mortgage loan numbers, computer passwords, and other important information to make it easier on your executors during probate.*

Probate is a legal process that occurs when someone dies to determine what to do with their assets. The last thing you'll want to inflict on your loved ones is an unresolved situation. Ideally, the process should take six months to a year. But if you haven't paved the way to smooth execution ahead of time, it can drag on for years. Laws vary from state to state. For example, you might be able to sell a loved one's home to settle any debts. Not having a financial plan in place can be an emotional catastrophe for a family when they are already in mourning and distress. Putting measures in place to alleviate such pressure is a final gift you can provide your heirs.

Make a will!.

Making a will is worth the expense, even if you don't have a lot of assets. My wife and I both have wills that include provisions

* A book by a former college professor, Joel Larus, *The Final Gift: Creating a Record of Vital End-of-Life Information*, is an excellent, helpful tool.

for our daughters' care in case we die before they are adults. Because Athena and I believe that Chaz and Camille, as teenagers, were old enough to learn about money matters, we have explained our wills to them. We have had conversations with them reviewing all of our family's assets, so they have a clear understanding of our financial situation and our wishes for their future.

For example, we own a few rental properties. I don't care what they decide to do with them once we're gone. But they are never to sell the summer home in Tifton. My reasoning: no matter what life throws at you; you will always have a place to stay.

$ $ $ $ $

Chapter 20

$IGNIFICANT OTHER$
AND MONEY

I've saved discussing money and spouses for last because I have found it the most challenging aspect of my life. As American parenting expert John Rosemond has said, "Raising children is easy. Marriage is hard. You can't say to your spouse, 'Go to your room—one…two…three.'" And expect a positive outcome.

Whether married, with a significant other, or in a loose, long-term relationship, money or the lack thereof is often at the center of discontentment or disagreements. Financial issues can become the flashpoint for deeper flaws in the relationship. They might not rise to the surface if there is plenty of money to purchase a new home, car, jewelry, and other sundries or take a vacation. On the other hand, when there is only talk of debt and making ends meet, it can be difficult to be affectionate with each other.

As I mentioned before, two years after Athena and I got married and lived under the same roof again, we were still seeing eye to eye on all financial matters—use of our credit card, taking out loans and making large purchases. When we were apart during my transfers and deployments, she did not have to check with me to purchase most things she needed or desired. But once we were together again, she felt she was losing her financial freedom. I was trying to manage our money the best way I knew how, but to her, my controlling decisions about how we spent it seemed like I was controlling her. She would go along to get along, because she believed I would not change my outlook if she disagreed. Given how categorical I can be at times, she probably had a point.

From 2005 to 2006, when Chassidy was born and I was deployed in Iraq, I loosened the financial strings and agreed to let Athena call some of the shots on her own again. After I returned home, emotionally shaken by how fragile our lives were, I went on my famous shopping spree. I failed spectacularly when I tried to return to our former way of doing the family finances.

We bought a new car, a 2007 Chrysler 300. We purchased a home in Tifton, Georgia, in addition to our house in Washington State. When we moved to northern Virginia in the summer of 2008 while expecting our second daughter, I continued my profligate spending. Although we were doing well financially, we could have been doing much better.

From 2010 to 2011, when I was deployed to Afghanistan, I once again failed to invest and save money from my promotion to Major. At the same time, it seemed that Athena never had enough money to cover daily household expenses. I could not understand why, but she was home alone with the girls, so I sent her whatever she asked for. Financially, we were not in the same chapter anymore, much less on the same page.

Her sister, who was staying in our house in Tifton, couldn't cover the mortgage, so I took care of that, too. Although her monthly contributions didn't amount to much, I should have applied them to pay down the principal more quickly, but I didn't.

After a serious disagreement with Athena, her sister moved out, leaving us in the lurch. Fortunately, it happened while I was back in the States on my mid-tour leave. We cleaned out the house and, using my extra earnings from Afghanistan, redid the flooring and countertops and bought furnishings. It felt good to have something to show for the extra money I made while deployed.

When I returned from Afghanistan for good, I bought another pick-up truck, a blue Ford F150. Having endured my love affair and the financial debacle with Big Nastee, Athena disagreed and tried to reason with me. But I was deaf to all arguments and made some unfortunate statements, notably, "I was the one deployed, not you." I felt I deserved the vehicle and plowed ahead. I named the Ford "Blu M@j!c" (pronounced "Blue Magic").

Having this pick-up truck has been a godsend. When we purchased two duplexes as investment properties, they needed a lot of renovation, and Blu M@j!c became a workhorse. We hauled debris to landfills after demolitions and picked up building supplies to deliver to the site. Since then, I've used the truck to transport all kinds of things. Of course, I couldn't predict those benefits ahead of time. When I bought it, I just wanted it.

At times, I still try to justify my act of defiance because of the things we have been able to do with Blu M@j!c, but that doesn't make up for the fact that my uncompromising behavior was a watershed moment in Athena's and my financial lives. I established a precedent for our practice to this day by insisting that she does not get a vote on how I spend "My Money." Although I never uttered those exact words, my actions all but shouted them in her face. It wasn't what was best for our relationship and started us down a path of dealing with our finances separately.

When Athena wanted a cosmetic medical procedure done, I suggested she finance it rather than pay cash or draw on her investments. However, she was adamant about using her assets because it was "Her Money." I did not argue or ask to see any receipts.

We were still following the practice established from the outset of our marriage—splitting bills for the mortgage, childcare, and utilities and shared a credit card so one person could not use it without the other knowing about it. But we didn't make any financial plans or chart an economic course for the family. I was doing quite well because I had paid off Blu M@j!c, so I had a surplus of cash in my account. But I did not use it to increase our investments and pay down the mortgage on our second home. I considered it was spending money and was happy to splurge.

A couple of years after we relocated to Georgia, I felt that I had reached the apex of my career and started to think about retiring. By then, Athena and I were barely in the same book regarding finances. She was doing her thing, and I was doing mine.

To her credit, Athena was educating herself about finances via podcasts and began to increase her investments. I was stuck in

Cash-Is-King mode and did not want my money tied up. With financial investments, the money is there, but you must meet specific criteria before using it. I could always borrow against what I had invested, but I didn't want to do that. It was my money, and I wanted it available at any time, without strings attached.

It took reading J. L. Collins' book for me to adjust my financial mindset about that.

Now that both Athena and I have retired from the military—Athena finished in September of 2021—we continue to operate on separate tracks. Even though we are named on each other's bank account, Athena has her credit card and I have mine. That has not created difficulties for us. She pays her bills; I pay mine.

Still, there are times when I feel that we are at a financial crossroads for the foreseeable future because I don't know how to chart a new fiscal course for us to move forward together. I don't know anything about the investments Athena has made on her own. I don't know the names of the companies or the investment products. I don't even know if I'm the beneficiary.

At the same time, I feel like I play a big part in her ability to invest because I put money into our joint savings anytime I have extra. I have purchased ceiling fans for the bedrooms, LED light fixtures for closets, microwaves, and a concrete-coated sun room and patio for our home to enhance its value. When we bought the two duplexes, I used my money for renovations. So, I get frustrated because I feel that Athena is not willing to sacrifice to the same degree I do.

By now, I'm sure you've cottoned to the fact that I am not the most patient person in the world. As a result, many financial conversations between Athena and me have been fraught with tension. I get especially frustrated by our different approaches. For example,

I answer if she asks me about a financial transaction. But if I inquire about one of hers, she deflects. It feels like 21 questions, and if I don't ask just right, I don't get an answer.

What I desire most is a consistent process to work through financial matters and her willingness to sacrifice and pay attention to the little things so we can move forward together. If you know you can cover the cost, don't ask me for half the money. Just go ahead and pay for it. I will always put any extra money into the family coffers because it's extra money. I'm willing to delay vacations and dream gifts to achieve financial freedom. However, the sacrifices cannot be one-sided.

For quite a while, I felt angry and betrayed that Athena didn't love me the way she used to. Fortunately, I had an epiphany at some point: Love and finances are two different things. Fundamentally, love has nothing to do with money. I've been conflating the two. Love is about being united, but having separate finances does not mean love has changed.

> **It's best to keep your financial issues
> separate from your love language.**

Through a professional contact, it was suggested that Athena and I take the Kolbe assessment. The test measures the instinctive ways that individuals take action. People have different approaches when starting projects, facing challenges, or getting jobs done. None of them are inherently wrong, but people with other profiles who don't know that can get into conflict about how to go about it. The benefit of the Kolbe is that you can appreciate the difference and work together more effectively once you understand your own and someone else's approach. It enables one to remove emotions from the equation and not blame the discord on the other individual's personality, intelligence, or social style.

During the debrief, the narratives from the assessments were spot on. Athena needs time to research a topic before she takes action. She does not like deadlines imposed on her, especially by me. On the other hand, I do not need much information to execute when I imagine the desired outcome. I move forward quickly—some would say, fly by the seat of my pants—but I appreciate being part of a team.

This explains some of our differences in our approach to money matters. Athena is more cautious and wants considerably more information than me to make decisions.

Here is an example of how that pans out. When our tax preparer failed to file our LLC's taxes from 2015-2019, we incurred several tax penalties. He is not a CPA, although he specializes in tax preparation, as well as immigration services. It seems that he did not have much experience filing taxes for LLCs, even though we provided the required documents. After discussing the matter with him, he agreed to pay the $4,800 fine for the previous year. But that left two years of earlier tax penalties. The IRS transferred those fines to a collection agency. Now, doesn't that beat all? The IRS needs a collection agency?

I was eager to settle the account immediately. I expressed my concern to Athena about the tax preparer failing to provide the funds quickly for the previous penalty. If he refused to pay, we would have to leverage our accounts. But Athena wanted time to contact the IRS and review the tax documents from the penalty years. She created a spreadsheet to give her a clearer picture of the situation. She also sought advice from a sorority sister who is a CPA and felt that we should all sit down with the tax preparer to discuss the matter. Athena had us in a holding pattern for a few extra days. I believe it's prudent to be patient, but not when interest is accruing by the day. We'd have to pay the IRS regardless; the additional information would not reduce the bill. Fortunately, the tax preparer provided the funds, and I remitted the payment to the IRS.

The next matter to resolve was whether we'd continue to do business with him. For me, he was the long pole in the tent. But, as the saying goes, "Better the devil you know than the one you don't." Because he paid the penalties to the IRS without complaint, we decided to retain his services.

I also have a less rigorous approach to certain informal money matters. For example, quality moonshine is hard to acquire. Moonshine is taboo these days because you can buy it from a liquor store, where it is regulated and taxed. But you can get homemade lightning from the hills of Kentucky, Tennessee, or Virginia, where cottage industries create high-quality products. When I come across some good shine during my travels, I inform close friends that I have some on hand and share the bounty. I never charge a transportation fee, so I don't make a profit from my efforts. These days, I would rather sell something to someone who could really use it at cost, especially if I am not doing anything with it.

Athena is the exact opposite. For her, any financial transaction should have an economic benefit. She believes her efforts should be rewarded.

The Kolbe test revealed why we are significantly at odds over money, principally regarding business. From her perspective, I am throwing money away. For me, it's an investment in people that will manifest in the future that is not cloaked with greenbacks.

As of this writing, I realize that Athena and I are on the same financial journey, just in different vehicles. We were in the same car at the outset, and I did most of the driving. Sometimes I would invite her to share driving duties. I preached teamwork because that's how we got to this point, although I didn't always act accordingly. Athena has charted a new route in her own vehicle without me on the passenger side. That caused much angst for me because I wanted to stick to the roads I knew and have her along for the ride.

> **There is no right or wrong way to handle money as a couple—jointly or separately can both work.**

The bottom line is that we continue to talk and try to understand how to move forward. We are a work in progress.

$ $ $ $

For no man who lives at all, lives unto himself.
He either helps or hinders all who are
anywise connected with him.

—Frederick Douglass

Chapter 21

MARRIAGE THOUGHT$

Money can't buy love, but it can damn sure finance it. I always longed to be married with kids. I wanted a nice house with a son and a daughter. My parents were not the typical married couple, but that is another story. There is no instructional manual for marriage, but I watched a lot of television as an adolescent, and what I saw stuck with me. I know Bill Cosby is persona non grata—and for good reason: his predatory behavior with women is inexcusable—but The Cosby Show was a comprehensive model for what a marriage could be. Cliff and Claire Huxtable parented with integrity and displayed their commitment and love for one another. Most importantly, there were only verbal disagreements, no physical fights, and matters were always resolved before an episode ended. That was how I envisioned marriage.

I seriously considered getting hitched to LPJ's daughter a year after I graduated college. But she was undecided about her career pursuits. She was a biology major but didn't want to teach or pursue a career in the medical field. After she graduated, she returned home and lived with her parents for a while. I was only 23 years old. I struggled to take care of myself, and I would have to provide for her, which was a significant concern for me. As it turned out, the relationship didn't last.

It's funny because the current advice I give young people is, "Don't let money impact your decision to marry. If the person matters that much to you, fight to keep them in your life." Tough talk, I know, and even a tad hypocritical, but it's been my stance because of that experience. It played a significant role in my decision to marry Athena. I would not allow a lack of money, limited time, or distance to distort my vision of growing old with Athena.

Today, I liken my marriage to a professional sports contract. The National Basketball Association (NBA) has a 10-day contract option. If you perform well enough, it can be extended and yield a multi-year contract. From my perspective, my marriage is on an annual contract. That's not to imply that we will call it quits on each other, but our interests change from year to year. I must be in tune with that. My initial actions to attract her and her efforts to snare me are memories. That means the marriage cannot be on cruise control. I know now that marriage is like a garden that must be tended. I must do my part.

I've learned that marriage is not always 50/50, and it doesn't have to be to achieve success. Despite a union, each person has a unique set of gifts. One person may make more money than the other. Traditionally, the man is expected to be the breadwinner and covers all expenses. Some couples put their money together and cover the costs accordingly. Some people cover expenses based on a percentage of income. Thus, it's essential to do what works for your situation and adjust as necessary because things change. Athena and I generally cover expenses based on who makes the most money. We divvy bills accordingly.

Bottom Line: If two people are married, they should be better together than apart.

I learned that marriage is like writing a never-ending story. The previous chapters don't have any bearing on what the subsequent chapters produce. It's best to leave prior emotions in previous chapters and not hope they carry on to the next. Marriage is a courageous act that requires you to treat each day as a new page to write your story. Your characters are not predestined from page to page but are subject to change with each new entry.

$ $ $ $ $

For many retirement is a time of personal growth which becomes the path to greater freedom.

—Robert P. Delamontague

Chapter 22

RETIREMENT BENEFIT$

I did not join the Army to retire with a pension. I was not concerned about promotions, special assignments or being Airborne qualified. At the time, I planned to complete my four-year obligation after college and transition to the civilian world. When I put on the uniform, I only had two specific goals. I wanted to be assigned to a unit in Germany and purchase a BMW car from Europe. I was not interested in "Being All I Could Be" in those days. Turns out, I never served in Germany or purchased a BMW from Europe.

I liken my service time to the military version of "Simon Says." The Army says you will train in California for 30 days, you train in California for 30 days. The Army says deploy to Iraq for a year, you deploy to Iraq for a year. The Army says you need inoculations to prepare for future operations, you take the shots.

As the saying goes, "The days are long, but the years will be short," meaning "time flies," and before I knew it the Army became a 20-year career. By my fifteenth year of service, I realized that retirement was within my purview.

In 2016, I was promoted to Lieutenant Colonel. It put me in an excellent financial position.

I decided to compete for Battalion Command selection, which would make me competitive to become a Colonel. But one of my supervisors informed me that my file wasn't strong enough and that I would probably not be picked. With dim prospects of achieving a higher rank, I adjusted my financial and career goals. Army regulations would have allowed me to serve as a Lieutenant Colonel until 2027. But I did not want to stick around to be a flunky. My evaluations would not have mattered—I was a good soldier and did what I was ordered to do—and I would have been considered "a man with no legs."

By then, I believed taking control of my circumstances was essential. So, I decided to retire. I have no regrets about that.

> **It's OK not to achieve your goals.**
> **Having something to strive for is motivation enough.**

Military retirement is based on your years of service and 2.5% of your highest 36-months base pay, referred to as High 3. The military transitioned to the Blended Retirement System in January 2018. The new system ensures that service members can receive good retirement benefits without doing 20 years. I benefitted from both systems. Although I officially retired in 2019, I was also grandfathered in under High 3.

Initially, the most challenging adjustment for me was the transition to a single payment on the first of every month. After years of active duty, when I was paid on the first and fifteenth of every month, I now had to become creative and stretch my dollars and, at times, even make them do gymnastics to get to the end of the month.

The good thing about the monthly disbursement is that it reinforces my financial discipline. I prioritize my purchases and only rarely indulge in frivolous expenses. Like most people who own a house, the mortgage is my largest expense, but I still invest a significant sum of money every month to benefit my daughters' future.

The GI Bill created after September 11 is a significant benefit for the military. When the Post-9/11 Veterans Educational Assistance Act of 2008 went into effect on August 1, 2009, it provided educational benefits to service members and their families. If service members do not use the benefits, they can transfer them to a family member. In my case, I gave them to Chassidy. As a result, she has something already in the kitty for college.

In 2017, we purchased our home in Columbus, Georgia. I had paid off my cars, so I used my money to upgrade our residence. I repaired the fence, added driveway space, and completed a sun room. I was planning on taking a Junior Reserve Officers' Training position at one of the local high schools. However, when I received my first retirement and disability payments, I made enough money to cover expenses. It helped that Athena was still serving, so I decided to take a year off before I thought seriously about my future.

Well, one year has turned to four years. I have yet to have a serious conversation with myself or anyone else about career opportunities. I enjoy moving at my own pace, not being tied to a computer or having to answer my phone. Most of all, I love dealing with people on my terms. I don't give out my phone number or email address unless it's necessary to conduct business. I am interested in running for City Council to try to be a part of the solutions for the city instead of talking about problems all day. I have contemplated going back to school to pursue a master's degree in Public Administration. But the longer I'm unemployed, the more likely I won't go back to work fulltime. I certainly won't commit to anything full-time until my daughters are in college. That way, I won't be as distracted and can focus my energy as required. Chaz will begin applying to college this summer, and Camille enters high school next year.

$ $ $ $ $

Po$tlude

Life, with all its ups and downs, happens to all of us. Cherish the good times because there will always be difficulties and challenges –illness, financial hardship, or death of someone important to you. They will knock you down, but it is how you respond that really matters.

When it comes to finances, don't confuse money with life. I always wanted money to get the things that caught my attention in my early years. As I made more money, I purchased more stuff. My relationship with the mighty dollar was: The more you make, the more you spend.

As of this writing, that relationship has taken a 180-degree turn. I am approaching the half-century mark, and my materialistic desires have subsided somewhat. I prioritize expenditures based on my needs more than my wants. I no longer have the urge to indulge in the latest technological marvel or the most recent fashion trend. I prefer to use my money to make memories with friends and family. Memories through special events, travel, or fine dining. At this point in my life, I think of money as a tool to leverage and invest in myself and others.

I make one exception: wristwatches. I own more than twenty. They are my weakness. I'll always be in the market for an attractive timepiece. I know I can only wear one at a time, but they are accessories to my wardrobe. The event determines which one adorns my wrist. To my credit, I am a novice watch repairer, so I can replace batteries and make minor repairs as needed.

I always hear about what people would do if they had so much money, and how life would be so different. They use their money to purchase things to make them happy, but the feeling dissipates when they receive the receipt from the purchase.

I've learned that you cannot change someone's mentality about money, no matter how much or little they have. It's the biggest reason so many athletes, entertainers, and lottery winners go broke. They make poor people's decisions and refuse to learn from others' mistakes.

No matter how much you try to dissuade someone from a useless purchase, all the logic in the world won't work. It costs to maintain things—boats, houses, airplanes (for small propeller enthusiasts), and, yes, Four-Wheelers. It's one of the reasons I've never purchased a home with a swimming pool. Maintaining it is a significant expense, and you can't use it year-round, only for a few months out of the year.

I've learned that your financial portfolio is no one else's concern. At the same time, there is no need to "count someone else's pockets." Be thankful for what you have, repay borrowed money expeditiously, and help others accordingly. There is nothing wrong with wanting what someone else has, but never covet someone else's belongings. In that moment, your relationship with money becomes corrupted because you want money to be someone else. If you genuinely desire to improve your lot, ask for advice and do something about it.

That's an important lesson because, in my experience, I've learned that most people don't want help. They would rather fail miserably and wallow in their shame before accepting help from others. People have become so hardwired that they refuse to unlearn what they think they know in order to learn something new. Most people consider change bad, but change is inevitable. If you resist it, you merely exist rather than live a full life. At times, I think we are all existing, but to remain in that state for too long could lead to a slow death.

My focus for the next five to ten years is to take care of my mom, enjoy my marriage to Athena, and support my daughters, putting them on the path to becoming responsible adult citizens. I consider a responsible adult is someone who is employed, has access to quality health care, understands a variety of investment vehicles, and has the ability and discipline to save money. I came to the table late with that realization and development. I hope Chaz and Camille can get there earlier.

The other important part of living is to take pleasure in activities and events.

I want to continue to enjoy HBCU football games. I plan to purchase an RV so Athena and I can visit the 50 states before we turn 50. We also intend to visit Africa and Greece. For spring break this year, we want to take our daughters to the Bahamas. In December, Athena and I have our twentieth wedding anniversary. To celebrate, we are planning to go to Grenada and maybe have an event to renew our vows.

I am using my financial portfolio to assist extended family members in achieving their goals. I plan to complete all major renovations for the several properties in my real estate portfolio. I will continue to chart my course toward financial independence by paying off the mortgage of my primary home. I want to be more philanthropic to causes that matter to me. That includes increasing my donations to Hampton University, veteran organizations, and other nonprofits that assist disadvantaged young people.

Looking back on my military service, I realize that one of the benefits was that the motivation and purpose were innate because I volunteered to serve. Military life also taught me the importance of integrity and communication. Oral and written communication can reduce friction and lead to shared understanding. Integrity is another matter. It's one thing to be inept or fail to look the part, but lacking integrity is a career killer. I witnessed out-of-shape and incompetent individuals who survived the Army but not anyone who lacked integrity. One cannot earn integrity, but one can surely give it away.

I transitioned to civilian life with the following traits: a love of running, extra work, sacrifice, integrity, and communication. Unfortunately, I had to leave the motivation and purpose in the Army when I retired. Developing it on my own is an ongoing challenge.

Pablo Picasso said, "The meaning of life is to find your gift. The purpose of life is to give it away."

As a civilian, I'm assembling my gifts to ascertain my purpose for the next chapter of my life.

$$\$ \ \$ \ \$ \ \$ \ \$$$

CARLO$' FINANCIAL
AND LIFE LE$$ON$

(mostly learned)

Never cosign a loan with anyone, especially a family member.

When you give people something, it belongs to them to do with as they please.

Don't let emotions run wild in conflicts with family and friends.

Keep your cool during conflicts with others.

If you can, invest a portion, however small, in a mutual fund or equivalent.

Coin change adds up, so collect and deposit.

If at all possible, get a bank account.

If you love someone, keep talking—nicely—until you find out what you need to know about each other.

Do what is necessary to eat well.

Don't let the behavior of others get in the way of friendship. And don't be a moocher.

When faced with death, saving money becomes the least concern.

Unless you're insanely rich, limit your budget for toys to $500.

Have a big garage to park the toy you can't use.

Saving money is always good, but the bottom line isn't always the most important thing.

Always have a sledgehammer handy for demolition.

While caring for someone, it's essential to know all the facts about their money and actively participate in any financial decision.

When money is in play, it is prudent to have a contract, especially if it involves a family member.

If you are the primary caregiver for someone,

It's nobody else's business what you do with their money.

A life insurance policy is a must.

If you are serious about creating generational wealth.

Make a will!

Keep your financial issues separate from your love language.

There is no right or wrong way to handle money as a couple—jointly or separately can both work.

It's OK not to achieve your goals.
Having something to strive for is motivation enough.

$ $ $ $

ACKNOWLEDGMENT$

I am thankful for my friends, relatives and colleagues that listen to my stories with more than polite interest and attention. There are too many to name and I don't want to leave anyone out, but their belief in me empowers me to write. They don't know it, but their questions and comments keep me on task anytime I embark on a new manuscript.

I want to give a life-size shout out to my editor, Chris Angermann. I was going to discard this manuscript without giving it the light of day. As the saying goes, make them tell you NO. But although the draft was more jagged than rough, Chris saw value in it. I cannot praise him enough for his encouragement, professionalism, friendship and mentorship.

Finally, thanks to the four ladies that live under my roof: my wife Athena, my mom, Vyaleen, and my daughters Chassidy and Camille. They don't always provide the best environment for me to create, but they know when to give me space. I love y'all for that.

Educate, Evaluate and Elevate.

$ $ $ $ $

$HORT BIBLIOGRAPHY AND RESOURCE$

Baradaran, Mehrsa, *The Color of Money: Black Banks and the Racial Wealth Gap*.

Collins, J.L., *The Simple Path to Wealth: Your Road Map to Financial Independence and a Rich, Free Life*.

Desmond, Matthew, *Evicted: Poverty and Profit in the American City*.

Larus, Joel, *The Final Gift: Creating a Record of Vital End-of-Life Information*.

The Kolbe Index assessment is available online at *https://www.kolbe.com*.

You can take the test yourself and get results via the website, but I recommend using a Kolbe consultant who can explain the finer details and wrinkles of the results.

$ $ $ $ $

Carlos A. Lock is a native of Jackson, Mississippi. He graduated from Hampton University with a Bachelor of Science in Finance. He has a Master of Arts in Higher Education from the University of Louisville.

Serving in the U.S. Army, Carlos had two combat tours to Afghanistan and Iraq and retired as a Lieutenant Colonel. He was a certified logistics professional and earned several awards, most notably the Bronze Star. He credits his military service for much of his financial know-how and discipline.

Carlos finished his Army career in Columbus, Georgia, where he lives with his wife, mother and two daughters. He is the author of *Black College Football: The Game That Time Forgot.*